THE *New* SMART

HOW NURTURING CREATIVITY
WILL HELP CHILDREN THRIVE

DR. TERRY ROBERTS

FOREWORD BY HOWARD GARDNER

TURNER PUBLISHING COMPANY

Turner Publishing Company
Nashville, Tennessee
www.turnerpublishing.com

The New Smart: How Nurturing Creativity Will Help Children Thrive

Cover design: Rodrigo Corral
Book design: Tim Holtz

Library of Congress Cataloging-in-Publication Data Available Upon Request

9781684423712 Paperback
9781684423729 Hardcover
9781684423736 Ebook

Printed in the United States of America
17 18 19 20 10 9 8 7 6 5 4 3 2 1

The winds of change are blowing wild and free.
—Bob Dylan

Smart people are a dime a dozen, and many
of them don't amount to much.
What matters is creativity, the ability to apply
imagination to almost any situation.
—Walter Isaacson

To Jesse, Margaret, and Henry—
in so many ways, the inspiration for this book.

CONTENTS

FOREWORD

If you were to come to my office at the Harvard Graduate School of Education, where I have taught for decades, you'd see two walls covered with framed letters. Nearly all of these missives are from teachers of mine—some of whom I worked alongside for years, others of whom I related to chiefly by mail. While it may appear that I am showing off my acquaintance with some well-known scholars, my goal with this display is different. Any of us who presumes to add to the library of knowledge builds upon the ideas, the arguments, and the publications of those who have taught us. And we hope that, if they encounter our own thoughts, these letter writers, these teachers, will feel that they have done good work.

As the creator of the "theory of multiple intelligences" and as one who has written extensively about creativity, leadership, and education, I am pleased to be able to introduce Terry Roberts's book. Terry has taken some of my ideas, and those of many other authors and educators, and put forth an intriguing portrait of the kinds of minds that we will want and need to cultivate in the next decades. He shows how these minds combine various forms of intelligence and how, working both alone and with peers, individuals marshal these minds to solve vexing problems and to create new products. And going beyond an essay on mind in the cognitive sense, Terry includes as well discussions of emotions, personality, and the surrounding culture, including both schools and workplaces. If you want a sense of the challenges that face the young people of the future, and the ways in which we may help those youth to meet those challenges over the course of a lifetime of learning and a life-time of work, you will gain much from reading and pondering Terry Roberts's book.

Though the ideas in this book could conceivably be applied universally, it is in some ways a classically American book. It assumes that individuals will be free to do what they want to do, and that they will be encouraged, or at least allowed, to challenge orthodoxy and create something that is unanticipated, innovative, even paradigm-breaking. I hope, I pray that this world will continue, but in an era of rising authoritarianism, we cannot easily make that assumption. Also, with American optimism, this book assumes that uses of mind will be benign, but of course originality can proceed in many directions, some of them quite mischievous. And so I hope, I pray, that societies will have the wisdom to encourage innovation but also to discourage or outlaw "deployments of intelligences" that are destructive. In the spirit of friendship and collegiality, I encourage Terry Roberts, as his next assignment, to help us think through these issues that are global or universal in nature. I for one will be an eager reader of his thoughts on these crucial topics.

Howard Gardner
Cambridge, MA

INTRODUCTION

IS *SMART*
THE RIGHT WORD?
IF NOT, WHAT IS?

At an April 1864 address in Baltimore, Abraham Lincoln famously remarked that "the world has never had a good definition of the word liberty, and the American people, just now, are much in want of one." As a writer and speaker—indeed, as a humanist philosopher—Lincoln was extraordinarily sensitive to the subtle meanings of words and their not-so-subtle power. Lincoln went on to say:

> We all declare for liberty; but in using the same *word* we do not all mean the same *thing*. With some the word liberty may mean for each man to do as he pleases with himself, and the product of his labor; while with others the same word may mean for some men to do as they please with other men, and the product of other men's labor. Here are two, not only different, but incompatible things, called by the same name—liberty.

Simply stated, varying factions manipulated the meaning and function of this common word to achieve their own ends.

I believe that as a fragmented society in the first quarter of the twenty-first century we face a similar dilemma. I would argue that the world has never had a good definition of the word *smart*, and just now, we are much in need of one. Much in need because of the complex challenges that face us and our children—some of whom we have chosen to label *smart* and some of whom we have labeled otherwise. In essence, this book seeks to answer the following question: *Who will prove to be successful in this new and volatile age?*

We recycle the word *smart*—along with the companion words *bright, capable, gifted, clever*—without pausing to consider what we actually mean. One exception to this is when we are being deliberately manipulative, using the word as a means to our own ends when we praise our own and criticize others. To echo Lincoln, I believe we pay a stern price for our inattention and our manipulation of this common word. We face a volatile and uncertain future, and we need a new idea—and along with it, a new term—that will serve all of us well in the decades to come.

If the term *smart* is so worn out as a concept that it has ceased to mean anything, then where do we go for a workable definition of twenty-first-century capacity? What lies beyond intelligence?

We live in a profoundly fragmented world—a world in which meaning is devilishly hard to come by and prosperity equally hard to measure, whether in dollars and cents or quality of life. Furthermore, our children and grandchildren are facing a postmodern world on steroids, in which change is the only predictable constant and there are no guaranteed paths to success. Indeed, young women and men in their twenties casually report that they've never known a particularly stable world; they are used to cultural instability and social upheaval. In their world, neither static definitions of intelligence nor traditional ideas of training stand us in good stead. Rather, we need to reframe the question given what lies before us and come to terms with a different answer posited in a different language.

If the defining characteristic of life in the twenty-first-century developed world is constant and fluid change, then the predominant experience will be increasingly that of asynchrony—the sense of being slightly behind the curve if not out of step entirely. In Thomas Friedman's prescient 2005 book, *The World Is Flat*, which describes the new global economics, he prescribed "positive imagination" as the necessary response to such an unpredictable, seemingly unforgiving world (443).

In order to thrive—not just survive but *thrive*—in an environment both global and volatile, we human beings must be creative in a new and vitally different way. We will need a profile rather than a profession, and we will be defined by poetic license rather than prosaic rules. For all these reasons, I believe that *creative* is the new *smart*.

Why do I argue for *creativity* rather than *intelligence*, even an expanded definition of *intelligence*? Because the world before us no longer works according to established rules, and success is no longer measured by traditional metrics. Because, as you will see in the chapters that follow, there is no longer a single predictor of success in school or beyond, just as there is no certain pathway to prosperity across the long arc of your life—or your child's. We cling to the old-fashioned notion of intelligence at our peril. In this brave new world in which we live, we will be required to develop something more complex and certainly more fluid.

When we juxtapose what we know about the twenty-first-century experience, whether public or private, against what we now believe about the nature of intelligence and talent, a profile of creative individuals emerges. This profile helps identify those who will thrive in the twenty-first century:

○ *They will blend multiple intelligences in a way that might be described as synthetic or even symphonic.*

○ *They will be ambitious and focused without being self-obsessed.*

○ *They will value asynchrony and even seek it out.*

○ *They will use their own marginality to generate a novel perspective and new work.*

○ *They will exhibit a steadfast resilience in all phases of life.*

○ *They will be measured by what they produce over the course of their lives, not by any static notion of capacity or quotient.*

In the fractured environment of the twenty-first century, true success will be unique and unexpected—the result of a creative response to complex, shifting challenges. So how do we prepare? How do we educate ourselves and our children for life in 2050?

Part One

BEYOND INTELLIGENCE

CHAPTER 1

MULTIPLE INTELLIGENCES

In 1983, Harvard psychologist Howard Gardner published a groundbreaking study of what he termed *multiple intelligences*. In *Frames of Mind*, Gardner not only summed up the history of social assumptions and scientific theories about intelligence but also went on to propose a much different lens through which we should view our own intellect and that of others.

In a key passage early in the book, Gardner juxtaposed two predominant "attitudes toward mind which have competed and alternated across the centuries." With tongue firmly in cheek, he christened the proponents of these two attitudes the hedgehogs and the foxes.

> The hedgehogs not only believe in a singular, inviolable capacity which is the special property of human beings: often, as a corollary, they impose the conditions that each individual is born with a certain amount of intelligence, and that we individuals can in fact be rank-ordered in terms of our God-given intellect or I.Q. So entrenched is this way of thinking—and talking—that most of us lapse readily into rankings of individuals as more or less "smart," "bright," "clever," or "intelligent." (7)

The foxes, on the other hand, believe not in one special property we might call intelligence, but in "the numerous distinct functions or parts of the mind." And furthermore, while "some of the foxes also tend to the innate and rank-ordering cast of thought . . . one can find many among them who believe in the altering (and ameliorating) effects of environment and training" (7).

As you'll see in the pages to come, the perspective of the hedgehogs is already outdated. It's high time we adopted the more flexible definition of intelligence advocated by the foxes—one that allows for multiple intelligences that exist within the creative individual.

THE NINE INTELLIGENCES

As Gardner develops his argument, he reveals himself as the granddaddy of all foxes—at least in our current henhouse—and famously goes on to identify seven, which later became nine, distinct intelligences:

- Linguistic
- Musical
- Logical-Mathematical
- Spatial
- Bodily-Kinesthetic
- Interpersonal
- Intrapersonal
- Naturalist
- Existential

The Howard Gardner who wrote *Frames of Mind* and other, later works like *The Mind's New Science* (1987) and *The Unschooled Mind* (1991) is at heart a scientist (although we will see him in a different guise later on), and he proposes rather strict criteria for a capacity or interest to be named an intelligence. In short, he doesn't nominate these nine lightly, and he is deliberate, even provocative, about naming them intelligences rather than tendencies or gifts.

It is well to remember that even this is not a complete list and that Gardner and others are constantly considering further nominees. It is also important to note, as Gardner himself takes pains to remind us, that these multiple intelligences are themselves an "idea," which is to say, a human construct. In this case, however, it is an idea that will lead us on to a prototype for twenty-first-century success.

My purpose here is not to rehash or rephrase Gardner's ground-breaking work in greater depth (others have done so), but rather to explore its implications for life in our fragmented age. First, a quick survey of what Gardner means by each of the nine intelligences.

Linguistic Intelligence

Linguistic Intelligence refers to the ability to use words effectively, even poetically, whether orally or in writing. Skilled practitioners include storytellers, orators, journalists, novelists, playwrights, editors, and poets. The primary symbol system is obviously language.

Musical Intelligence

Those with Musical Intelligence are able to appreciate and manipulate various forms of music effectively. Skilled practitioners include aficionados, composers, performers, and music critics. The primary symbol system includes the various elements of musical expression: rhythm, pitch, melody, and tone.

Logical-Mathematical Intelligence

This intelligence uses numbers as well as numerical formulas and operations effectively. It also includes the ability to recognize and manipulate patterns of all types, especially as they apply to geometric shapes. Skilled practitioners include scientists, coders, and accountants, as well as logicians. The primary symbol system includes the various mathematical languages, from primary numbers to algebra and calculus.

Spatial Intelligence

People with this type of intelligence perceive the visual-spatial world accurately, even creatively. Skilled practitioners include surveyors, cartographers, interior decorators, architects, physicists, and visual artists. This intelligence involves an appreciation for color, line, and shape in two-dimensional and three-dimensional space. The primary symbol system includes all the elements of visual art as well as many of the elements of geometry.

Bodily-Kinesthetic Intelligence

Someone with Bodily-Kinesthetic Intelligence uses the body gracefully and/or powerfully to compete athletically or express ideas or feelings, as well as using the hands to produce or transform things. Skilled practitioners include mimes, athletes, dancers, sculptors, mechanics, and craftspeople. The primary symbol systems (plural in this case) include the body itself as well as the material being crafted or manipulated by the hands.

Interpersonal Intelligence

Interpersonal Intelligence denotes the ability to perceive and interpret the moods, intentions, motivations, and emotions of other people and react appropriately. This intelligence includes the ability to respond effectively to a wide variety of interpersonal cues. Skilled practitioners include salespeople, teachers, coaches, and leaders of all kinds. The primary symbol system includes all sorts of communicative elements, including facial expression, body language, tone, voice, and gesture.

Intrapersonal Intelligence

Unlike Interpersonal Intelligence, which enables people to read the emotions of others, Intrapersonal Intelligence reflects the ability to cultivate an in-depth understanding of *the self* and act appropriately based on the knowledge. This intelligence can also include the development of insight into others based on an enhanced self-awareness. Skilled practitioners include psychologists, ministers, therapists, and entrepreneurs. The primary symbol system includes dreams (both waking and sleeping), self-assessment, and reflection.

Naturalist Intelligence

Those with Naturalist Intelligence have the ability to recognize and classify the numerous species—both flora and fauna—of an ecosystem and have an appreciation for the dynamic complexities of the natural world. (This environmental intelligence may also include an appreciation for the inanimate objects in an urban world.) Skilled practitioners include meteorologists, geologists, biologists, and naturalists of all kinds, as well as artists who depict the natural world. The primary symbol system includes the myriad elements—both seen and unseen—of the natural world, as well as the specialized language we use to define and describe that world.

Existential Intelligence

This intelligence indicates the ability to think conceptually about the larger philosophical and metaphysical questions of human existence, which often involves taking the long view of ephemeral events and placing them in a meaningful context. Skilled practitioners include philosophers, theologians, and historians. The primary symbol system of this intelligence is hard to define because existential insight can be expressed through a wide variety of linguistic and artistic media.

EVOLVING INTELLIGENCE

As a result of Gardner's work and that of other contemporary psychologists and neuroscientists, the long-held assumption that intelligence is a static element in an individual's makeup is slowly eroding. Because we have come to view the mind as more complex and more elastic, as capable of changing over the decades of an individual's life, we are beginning to give up the outdated notion of intelligence as a set, quantifiable quotient. Rather, we have increasingly come to see intelligence as multifaceted and fluid, which in turn means that individuals can evolve over the course of their lives, becoming more or less "smart" in a variety of ways.

The mind's new science (appropriately the title of Gardner's 1987 book) also means that the two areas in which we currently focus our schooling—linguistic and logical-mathematical—constitute a more narrow range of human potential and expression than we previously assumed. Ironically—and sadly—the educational community is perhaps the last large-scale enterprise in our society to respond to our new understanding of human capacity. This reluctance is in part because of the current addiction to the standardized testing of language and math skills to the exclusion of all others. For this reason, many efforts to classify students in elementary and middle school focus strictly on what is a narrow range of intellectual ability even for the schoolhouse—marginalizing or excluding Musical, Spatial, and Naturalist Intelligences, which are closely related to traditional school subjects. This narrow focus also largely ignores the personal intelligences as well as existential matters, which might have little to do with academics but everything to do with life. All this because we don't know how to measure these other vital ways of being "smart" via cost-effective, standardized tests.

As a result, employers across the United States and in foreign countries are hungry for graduates with communication, critical thinking, and teamwork skills in addition to increased technical savvy, but by and large our educational community hasn't yet caught up. This head-in-the-sand attitude on the part of the educational establishment continues despite the best efforts of reformers like Thomas Armstrong (through his book *Multiple Intelligences in the Classroom*) and the ever-charismatic Ken Robinson (who argues in *The Element* for students being allowed to find their unique passions). One of the reasons that the educational establishment hasn't responded more quickly to our changing understanding of intelligence is that our fundamental social attitudes toward who and what is "smart" are also lagging behind. What Gardner wrote in 1983 is still more or less true 34 years later: Too many "of us [still] lapse readily into ranking of individuals as more or less . . . 'bright,' 'clever,' or 'intelligent'"— especially when we're talking about young people.

Interestingly enough, however, there is a group in our society that is beginning to grasp the shifting landscape of success in school versus success in life: parents. In conversations across the world, parents are comparing the varied strengths and interests of multiple children and discovering that the sibling who is most successful at "playing the game" of school isn't necessarily the sibling who later excels in the work world or who is most comfortable in a fluid sociocultural landscape. They are also beginning to notice that a childhood and adolescence defined by one academic success after another under the tutelage of only the best teachers does not prepare their children for life in a profoundly nonlinear world.

The educational systems in many developed countries—the United States included—are even slower to adapt than they appear to be, because they prepare children and adolescents according to contemporary needs and values when the fact is that those children won't be adults in 2020. Rather, they will need to live and compete in 2040 and 50 and 60—perhaps even 2070 and 80. Obviously, we can't imagine the technical skills they will need. But we can imagine the full suite of intelligences they will need—and the creative ways in which they will be called on to integrate and demonstrate those intelligences. The first step in our exercise in imagination, then, is to admit that those who thrive will exhibit not just one form of intelligence but many.

CHAPTER 2

BLENDING INTELLIGENCES

In the introduction to his 2017 biography of Leonardo da Vinci, Walter Isaacson explains why he chose da Vinci as his topic after writing about the lives of Henry Kissinger, Benjamin Franklin, Albert Einstein, and Steve Jobs. Isaacson writes that he "embarked on this book because Leonardo da Vinci is the ultimate example of the main theme of my previous biographies: how the ability to make connections across disciplines—art and sciences, humanities and technology—is a key to innovation, imagination and genius." Da Vinci, like Isaacson's other subjects, was "wildly imaginative, passionately curious, and *creative across multiple disciplines*" (3, emphasis added).

He tags da Vinci as a "genius" and then goes on to argue that the label shouldn't distance Leonardo from the rest of us such that we can't relate to his life and work. His "genius," Isaacson argues, "was a human one, wrought by his own will and ambition. . . . Leonardo had almost no schooling and could barely read Latin or do long division" (3). Rather it was da Vinci's inexhaustible curiosity combined with an ability to blend his "studies of anatomy, fossils, birds, the heart, flying machines, optics, botany, geology, water flows, and weaponry" that fed his peculiar mind and personality. Even more the point, all of these "scientific explorations informed his art" (1–2).

Isaacson proceeds to describe how da Vinci's notebooks provide an extraordinary window into his ability to merge multiple disciplines and create out of that merger something that neither art nor science alone could have produced. As an example he cites a single page from the notebooks: "a large one, twelve-by-eighteen inches, that [da Vinci] composed in about 1490," that dramatically portrays Leonardo's myriad interests. There is a detailed portrait of an old man, a multitude of careful geometric drawings, the sketch of a mountain range, as well as "the trunk and branches of a leafless tree, which blend into [the old man's] toga and suggest the aorta and arteries of his blood system" (108–109). All of this imagery is accompanied by notes in da Vinci's curious backward handwriting. These elements—from art and mathematics and nature—flow in and out of each other almost as if parts of one extended vision, a web of sight and insight generated through Leonardo's stylus as his mind synthesized these varied elements. In essence, his creative mind blended multiple intelligences.

CREATORS TYPICALLY EXPRESS A COMBINATION OF INTELLIGENCES

If we transfer da Vinci's ability to think and create across disciplines into the frame provided by Howard Gardner's multiple intelligences, a startling new view of creativity and imagination emerges. It's not surprising that after exploring multiple intelligences in a series of books written during the 1980s, Gardner himself embarked on a trailblazing study of creative genius. His *Creating Minds* (1993) is "an anatomy of creativity seen through the lives of Freud, Einstein, Picasso, Stravinsky, Eliot, Graham, and Gandhi." In this book, he approaches the phenomenon of creativity by studying the lives of twentieth-century individuals who are universally recognized as creative in various fields of endeavor (psychology for Freud, physics for Einstein, dance for Martha Graham, and so on).

The result of this astonishing metabiographical study is what Gardner terms "a portrait of the exemplary creator," which synthesizes the common elements of the seven lives he studies. This portrait informs much of what will follow in this book (see especially chapter 3), but for now the most interesting element is one that Gardner discovered along the way. "A major assumption," he wrote, "has been that creators differ from one another in the kinds of intelligences that they exhibit; and indeed, each of the creators was selected because he or she was thought to exemplify one of the seven intelligences that I detailed in *Frames of Mind*."

But Gardner then goes on to "conclude that creators differ from one another not only in terms of their dominant intelligence but also in terms of breadth and the combination of intelligences" (363). Gardner discovered that creativity flows out of yoking multiple intelligences in the face of a problem or challenge. He provides a "rough summary" of intellectual strengths of his subjects:

Freud	linguistic, personal
Einstein	logical-spatial
Picasso	spatial, personal, bodily
Stravinsky	musical, other artistic
Eliot	linguistic, scholastic
Graham	bodily, linguistic
Gandhi	personal, linguistic

Note how even in describing the strengths of these creators, Gardner blends intelligences: The "personal" intelligences signify both Interpersonal as well as Intrapersonal, Eliot's "scholastic" certainly suggests a mix of academic disciplines, and Stravinsky's "other artistic" must contain everything from Bodily-Kinesthetic to Spatial in his staging of the ballet. And imagine for a moment if we added

Existential Intelligence to the list of possibilities (as Gardner did after *Creating Minds* was written); certainly Freud and Gandhi would qualify if not also Einstein and Eliot.

Gardner also discusses the sometimes dramatic weaknesses of the creators (for example, Picasso's interpersonal sadism), but the larger point here is that each of these seven prototypical creators—like da Vinci—merged separate intelligences in order to produce astonishingly new work. Freud even used his unique blend of intelligences to create an entirely new field of study, psychology, which along with psychoanalysis becomes the epitome of intrapersonal and interpersonal endeavor.

CYCLES OF CREATIVE EXPRESSION

In his massive, book-length study of creativity, Gardner also discovered something else: that creativity—unlike the traditional understanding of intelligence—evolves over the course of the creator's lifetime as she or he faces new and different challenges. In detailing the life cycles of his exemplary creators, he discovers something he calls "the shape of productivity":

> Without wishing to invest more magic in a numeral than is warranted, I have been struck throughout this study by the operation of the ten-year rule. These seven creators can be well described in terms of careers in which important events and breakthroughs occurred at approximately ten-year intervals. . . . As has already been well documented in studies of cognitive psychology, it takes about ten years for an individual to gain initial mastery of a domain. . . . The decade of an apprenticeship heightens the likelihood of a major breakthrough. (369–70)

What is fascinating about the patterns of productivity that Gardner discovered in these lives is that none of his archetypal creators were consistently productive over many years but rather started over after a significant breakthrough and recreated both themselves and their work. "The appeal of innovation rarely atrophies, but generally speaking, the subsequent breakthrough is of a broader and more integrative sort" (370). Several of Gardner's creators produce definitive works or events 30 years after their initial breakthrough, which argues for a lifetime of continuous growth and development in a cyclical pattern.

Certainly, this same dynamic and evolutionary view of individual creativity is supported by Isaacson's own lineup of creative personalities, whose productivity might also reflect the ten-year rule. What becomes clear in the study of either Isaacson's or Gardner's subjects is that creativity is a lifelong endeavor—if not an outright obsession—that is not built upon academic success or childhood giftedness. Indeed, a number of these men and women were poor students—if given access to education at all.

WHAT IS CREATIVE MASTERY?

What is wanted, then, is neither the prodigy nor the savant. Rather, success in the twenty-first-century world will belong to the masters who continuously reinvent themselves over the course of a lifetime—whether that reinvention occurs in ten-year cycles or not.

This idea of success as defined in multiple phases or chapters in an individual's life is vital because it underscores the primacy of lifelong study and productivity. In his introduction to *The Great Books of the Western World*, Robert Maynard Hutchins wrote that what is called for "is interminable liberal education" (52), and by liberal education, he means learning "to read, write, speak, listen, understand, and think. . . . To reckon, measure, and manipulate matter, quantity, and motion in order to predict, produce, and exchange" all over the course of a long lifetime (4). All of this begins to sound like ongoing growth and development in Gardner's multiple intelligences, even though Hutchins wrote these words in the 1950s, long before we even began to think of multiple *intelligences* rather than a single governing IQ.

What, then, is creative mastery? The prodigy is not the answer; a glance at the lives of Einstein, Franklin, Gandhi, and Graham prove this. Furthermore, academic giftedness (as currently defined) has little to do with later success, especially in a nonlinear world. The savant is not the answer, for striking ability within a single domain or through a single intelligence can carry an individual only so far. The specialist, regardless of field, is not the answer, for as Hutchins argued as early as the 1950s, specialization limits the mind while training it.

Mastery is the product of a lifetime. As Gardner discovered, it most often manifests itself in a personality that is "self-confident, alert, unconventional, hardworking, and committed obsessively to [the] work" (364). Furthermore, it manifests itself through product and performance rather than test scores; the proper blend of creativity and hardheadedness is exceedingly difficult to test but consistently productive.

———

Creative mastery in a fluid world—more specifically, success in our twenty-first-century world—involves blending multiple intelligences over a lifelong journey, through multiple cycles of invention and reinvention. It requires an ability to use and blend separate intelligences in response to each new challenge.

CHAPTER 3

THE PROFILE OF CREATIVITY

If I am right that success in a volatile world flows out of profile rather than profession, what, then, are the characteristics of that profile? Who are the creative personalities who will flourish during the next 50 years?

In the introduction, those individuals are summarized as follows:

- *They will blend multiple intelligences in a way that might be described as synthetic or even symphonic.*
- *They will be ambitious and focused without being self-obsessed.*
- *They will value asynchrony and even seek it out.*
- *They will use their own marginality to generate a novel perspective and new work.*
- *They will exhibit a steadfast resilience in all phases of life.*
- *They will be measured by what they produce over the course of their lives, not by any static notion of capacity or quotient.*

So far this profile is only a sketch. This chapter will help fill in the details that render it lifelike.

First, what does it mean for an individual to thrive? Freud is famously credited as saying that "love and work are the cornerstones of our humanness" and further that "work and love, that's all there is." This refrain has been picked up and tossed back and forth by any number of psychologists and sociologists, including

Mihaly Csikszentmihalyi in *Flow*. Perhaps there are other elements that contribute to human happiness or achievement (play, humor, spiritual enlightenment), but if we take these two phenomena—love and work—as fundamental, to thrive means to eventually experience prosperity in one or, more likely, both. This formula for fulfillment is especially challenging in a fractured age when the sources of love and work are both complex and volatile. To find profound love and meaningful work in this world requires truly creative individuals.

THEY WILL BLEND MULTIPLE INTELLIGENCES SYMPHONICALLY

In the first two chapters, we explored the idea of multiple intelligences and the way in which creative individuals often yoke those intelligences to solve complex problems. There is more to that process than first meets the eye. By definition, a given form of intelligence predisposes an individual to view the world a certain way and to process and communicate about that world with certain assumptions, often through a given language. The nature of professional specialization in our society often sharpens those views and assumptions by rewarding them. Thus, a young girl with a logical-mathematical frame of mind enjoys her math and science classes and eventually studies medicine. But it's not until she learns to listen to her patients and work *with* them rather than *on* them that she finds reward in being a physician. In short, it's not until she discovers a latent skill for interpersonal relations and merges a newfound passion for people with her long-term passion for science that she becomes an effective doctor.

This sort of midcareer adjustment is not uncommon, but other, more unusual combinations produce even more creative results. Both Gardner and Isaacson reflect on how Einstein played the violin to free his mind while struggling to envision relativity. In his book titled *The Innovators*, about those who "created the digital revolution," Isaacson profiles Ada Lovelace, who in the nineteenth century fused the literary sensibility of her father, Lord Byron, with her mother's passion for mathematics to imagine an early computer. As a result, she is often applauded as the first person to visualize the full potential of a practical computing machine. The list could go on and on, but the larger point is that the creative genius is the least susceptible to the false god of specialization and can therefore synthesize varied intelligences in a way that is profoundly greater than the sum of its parts.

Da Vinci used fantastically detailed drawings to explore mechanical and scientific problems just as he studied optics, anatomy, and mechanics to inform his paintings. Eventually the three or even four intelligences involved—Logical-Mathematical, Spatial, Bodily-Kinesthetic, Naturalist—merged into one symphonic intelligence that was uniquely characteristic of a single individual.

It is important to note, however, that this type of fully integrated, fully realized creative personality is self-made, not born. It is the result of years of disciplined effort.

THEY WILL BE AMBITIOUS AND FOCUSED WITHOUT BEING SELF-OBSESSED

The creative personalities described here are not just ambitious in ways defined by existing society; they tend rather to want to improve that society or redefine its definition of success. Their focus comes from a desire to see further and understand more than those around them, combined with the willingness to outwork others in order to delve beneath the surface of things.

One unfortunate result of this intense desire to know is an obsession with the quest. In *Creating Minds*, Gardner describes the exemplary creator that he synthesized out of his seven models: "E.C. works nearly all the time, making tremendous demands on herself and on others, constantly raising the ante. In William Butler Yeats's formation, she chooses perfection of the work over perfection of the life. She is self-confident, able to deal with false starts, proud and reluctant to admit mistakes" (362). In short, not all creators are willing to compromise their desire for knowledge and productivity with the needs of those around them, and we might easily accuse them of selfishness—if not self-obsession.

But given that we are imagining a future in which both we and our children grow into this role, let's assume that it's possible to achieve a kind of conscious balance. That we can be ambitious for the work without becoming immune to family or friends. That we can put our hands around a new idea (figuratively speaking) without losing all contact with others. That we can reinvent ourselves and the world around us without becoming a stranger to our loved ones.

Is it possible to be both creative and humble? Possessed by a vision or an idea and still live happily in family or community? Gardner's research suggests not. He writes:

> I have reluctantly concluded that these characterizations [focus and desire] may traditionally have been taken in too positive a way. That is, the self-confidence [of the creative personality] merges with egotism, egocentrism, and narcissism: each of the creators seems highly self-absorbed, not only wholly involved in his or her own projects, but likely to pursue them at the cost of other individuals. (364)

Gardner notes that of his seven archetypes, Gandhi, Stravinsky, Graham, and Freud were at least "difficult toward others," and Picasso was "frankly sadistic."

On the other hand, Gardner would be the first to say that not all creative individuals fit this misanthropic mold. Einstein and Eliot were not difficult; they mostly just wanted to be left alone. And when we expand our pool of examples to include gregarious souls like Benjamin Franklin and Leonardo da Vinci, a different portrait emerges—that of someone who is capable of fellowship, family life, and even love. Indeed, there seems to be a creative personality who has the ability to turn off his or her ego and lay down the work long enough to enjoy communal life.

As Doris Kearns Goodwin (in *No Ordinary Time*) and others have recorded, during World War II Franklin Roosevelt developed an unusual daily ritual. He insisted on a predinner cocktail hour for himself and his staff, during which he served as bartender. Topics related to politics in general and the war in particular were forbidden, in order to let some light into dark and challenging times. FDR was as ambitious and focused as any of his contemporaries, his creative powers fully engaged, and yet he recalled how to mix—and enjoy—an old-fashioned.

THEY WILL VALUE ASYNCHRONY

Gardner's psychological and biographical research clearly suggests that creative personalities thrive when they are out of step with the cultural or professional mainstream. He writes that "the theme of marginality pervades" their lives:

> Some of the creators were distinctly marginal by accident of their birth: Einstein and Freud as Jews in German-speaking countries, Graham as a woman in a male-oriented world. Others were marginal because of where they came to live, by choice or by necessity: the Indian Gandhi abroad in the British empire; the Russian Stravinsky in Western Europe

and the United States; the American Eliot in London; the
Spaniard Picasso in Paris. (368)

More important, each of Gardner's creators "used his or her marginality as a leverage in work. . . . Whenever they risked becoming
members of 'the establishment,' they would again shift course to
attain at least intellectual marginality."

If we expand this sample of creators beyond Gardner's seven,
we immediately recall Franklin abroad in France and da Vinci, who
moved from Florence to Milan, back to Florence, back to Milan,
to Rome, and finally to France as employment and opportunity
led him.

This theme of the geographical and cultural expatriate—James
Baldwin living much of his adult life in France where his imagination
ran free—is a constant in creative lives. Think of Jane Goodall, who
left her life in England and found her life in Tanzania. Where geographical displacement doesn't occur, cultural or social displacement
often does. It may well be that creative individuals seek out marginality because its opposite—the assumptions and rules that govern a
given culture or field—is stifling when you live in the midst of it.
Almost 400 years ago, Francis Bacon described how "the force of
custom, copulate and conjoined and collegiate, is far greater" than
mere individual habit and was overwhelming except for the most
exceptional minds. For this reason, imaginative individuals avoid the
crowd and gravitate to the margins. In this way, they can establish
a novel perspective and perform new work, uninhibited by mainstream values and constraints.

This comfort with and even desire for asynchrony is not belied
by the patterns that Malcolm Gladwell identified in his 2008 book,
Outliers: The Story of Success. As Gladwell takes care to point out, the
most successful members of our society aren't outliers in the sense

that they come to pass solely as a function of their unusual talent. He argues that success is not "a simple function of individual merit" but is most often the result of training and opportunity (33). Gladwell's thesis is certainly true in a world where we can predict the landscape in which our children will compete. The more uncertain that landscape, however, the more valuable is creativity and resilience. As we will see in chapter 7, we can honor Gladwell's call for more universal opportunity and better training by schooling all children and adolescents for flexibility and resilience. In other words, we need to prepare them for the inevitability of life on the margins.

Our creative personality, then, naturally seeks greater intellectual and psychological freedom and, for this reason, is willing to sacrifice much in order to attain—and later to keep—that freedom. Creative individuals typically view the loss of a job or the dissolution of a marriage as an opportunity rather than a defeat. They are more comfortable with movement than with stasis because change represents energy and potential. And finally, they view a challenge—especially a demanding and difficult one—with relish rather than dread.

THEY WILL USE THEIR OWN MARGINALITY TO GENERATE A NOVEL PERSPECTIVE

The individual who will thrive in 2050 will undoubtedly be a risk taker—for the simple reason that the prescribed path, which in many ways is the path of least resistance, will inevitably lead to dead ends.

In *The River of Consciousness*, psychologist Oliver Sacks (the author of *Awakenings*) included a long chapter on creativity. He wrote:

> Why is it that of every hundred gifted young musicians who study at Juilliard or every hundred brilliant young

scientists who go to work in major labs under illustrious mentors, only a handful will write memorable musical compositions or make scientific discoveries of major importance? Are the majority, despite their gifts, lacking in some further creative spark? Are they missing characteristics other than creativity that may be essential for creative achievement—such as boldness, confidence, independence of mind? (140)

Sacks goes on to say that after a lifetime of studying the vagaries of human personality, he believes "it takes a special energy, over and above one's creative potential, a special audacity or subversiveness, to strike out in a new direction once one is settled. It is a gamble as all creative projects must be, for the new direction may not turn out to be productive at all."

The key phrase in this prescription is that *special audacity or subversiveness.* By definition, creativity defies expectations, breaks rules, and ignores the status quo. It requires Sacks's special audacity simply because it takes more energy and more daring to go off road than to drive between the lines. Furthermore, creativity is defined, at least in part, by what it *isn't*, and what it isn't is the expected, the normal, the tried and true. Interestingly enough, it often requires a widely accepted set of standards against which to do its best work. Of Howard Gardner's seven archetypal creators, only Freud wasn't by definition subversive. Freud didn't react against an existing standard in a given field but rather created his own field, which is perhaps the most subversive act of all.

There is a sense, then, in which the typical twenty-first-century success story will not just take the path less traveled but often cut a new path entirely. And those who thrive in that world will always have an eye out for a new way through.

THEY WILL EXHIBIT A STEADFAST
RESILIENCE IN ALL PHASES OF LIFE

The second part of Oliver Sacks's rather wistful description of creativity is that the new way "is a gamble as all creative projects must be, for the new direction may not turn out to be productive at all." All creators fail—sometimes spectacularly.

However, they respond to failure with passion and persistence. Think of Thomas Wolfe, who probably wrote more bad prose than any other major American author and paid the critical price for it. Think of Freud, who was booed from the podium when he first presented his ideas on the subconscious mind at a scientific conference. Think of Marie Curie, who was not allowed to attend the University of Warsaw and was discouraged from pursuing a career in science simply because she was a woman. Think of Darwin, whose own father told him that he cared "for nothing but shooting, dogs, and rat catching" before he departed England on the *Beagle*. Think of Lucille Ball, who began studying to be an actress in 1927 and was told by her first drama instructor to "try any other profession."

Thomas Wolfe wrote *Look Homeward, Angel*, the classic American coming-of-age novel. Sigmund Freud introduced us to the inner workings of our own minds. Marie Curie won not one but two Nobel Prizes, the second after suffering the devastating death of her husband and collaborator. Charles Darwin revolutionized the way we think about the nature of time and the origin of species. Lucille Ball made us all laugh—at her and at ourselves.

There is a constant theme here. Creativity responds to discouragement and even outright rejection with renewed tenacity and vigor. Its standard reply to failure is to carry on, through a dogged faith in its own unique insight. Resilience is vital to the creative process and the creative personality, for it empowers the creative mind to generate new insight in response to discouragement.

THEY WILL BE MEASURED BY WHAT THEY PRODUCE OVER THE COURSE OF THEIR LIVES

We have lived for decades with the notion that intelligence can be measured on a test and assigned a number—a paradigm that is at best simpleminded and at worst destructive. Creativity, on the other hand, cannot be tested.

The creative personality often escapes schooling without ever having been identified as especially gifted or talented. Or, if caught up in the web of intelligence testing and labeling, it doesn't especially respond to the lockstep of contemporary schooling. Indeed, early identification and exposure to "gifted" programming is no predictor of success or happiness in adult life nor is it a marker for creativity.

Furthermore, those who do become remarkably productive as adults often do so despite early failures in school and other structured environments. In his book-length study of optimal human experience, simply titled *Flow*, Mihaly Csikszentmihalyi describes three outstanding examples of this phenomenon:

> Thomas Edison as a child was sickly, poor, and believed to be retarded by his teacher; Eleanor Roosevelt was a lonely, neurotic young girl; Albert Einstein's early years were filled with anxieties and disappointments—and they all ended up inventing powerful and useful lives for themselves. (235)

The relevant point here is that none of these individuals was successful in school—just the opposite—and yet each contained the seeds of remarkable resilience and invention.

Given that we can't test for the creative personality described in this chapter, then how do we measure our own creative capacity or that of our children? The simple answer is through unstandardized productivity and performance. In short, what does a given individual produce over the course of a life many decades long, often filled with disappointment and occasionally with despair? What does she or he build, create, design, write, invent, perform? That is the measure that matters.

It goes almost without saying that creative potential is not limited by gender, sexual preference, race, or ethnicity. In fact, where an individual is marginalized by any of these social or biological labels— think Martha Graham or Zora Neale Hurston—personal ingenuity and force may well be sharpened rather than blunted.

Finally, it is important to note that the creative personality can express itself in many different professional roles; creativity is not limited to the arts. It can manifest itself in engineering as well as painting, mathematics as well as music, politics as well as poetry. Furthermore, the creative personality who will thrive in the decades to come will exhibit this invention and resilience in many different aspects of life, personal as well as professional, private as well as public.

The next step in our imaginative quest is to reflect on why this particular individual—symphonic, ambitious, marginal, resilient, productive—will be so in demand in the decades to come.

CHAPTER 4

IN AN ASYNCHRONOUS WORLD

A quick review of the current bookshelf reveals two common ways of looking at the state of human society in the first quarter of this century. One is that our age is characterized by an increasingly fragile and dangerous mix of cultures driven by technological and economic forces almost beyond our control. According to this view, the world is economically flat, and most workers in developed countries are already competing with workers across the world. Furthermore, social and cultural change is steadily accelerating due to the dizzying pace of technological development. In other words, despite the best efforts of nationalist politicians and nativist commentators who cry out for stronger borders and simpler racial identification, globalization is coming. In fact, it's already here. It's here and most of us are not ready for it—either personally or professionally.

A second view offers a somewhat longer approach and a more optimistic perspective. This second take on human society is summed up in Steven Pinker's 2011 book, *The Better Angels of Our Nature: Why Violence Has Declined.* In this massive study, Pinker argues that—ephemeral news reports to the contrary—social violence has actually declined over the last several hundred years, and human society is slowly becoming more civil. Pinker cites dozens of statistics to support his view that even in times of war or other social upheaval, our reaction as a species is less violent than it was in previous conflicts. In essence, Pinker argues that there has been a recent and marked "reduction in violence at many scales—in the family, in the neighborhood, between tribes and other armed factions, and among major nations and states" and that somehow our recent "history has engaged our psychology" to produce more "peaceable societies" (xxiii).

Although these two views—one more pessimistic and the other more optimistic—have dominated the recent debates about the future, I'd like to propose a third, more nuanced approach that synthesizes both. In this view, human societies, like empires, rise and fall in more or less predictable patterns over thousands of years. Periods of relative peace and even prosperity occur in bastions of cultural cohesion in which we are protected from chaos by the unifying effects of political due process or religious belief. Periods of certainty and calm, however, never last and are followed by periods of what Jacques Barzun calls *decadence*, in which the unifying forces dissolve, leaving us with what feels like social and even moral chaos. What is different about our current, fragmented age is that our present decadence seems especially volatile due to global economic and technological forces. In short, this particular age of uncertainty is accelerating at warp speed, and 2050 is tomorrow.

Seen in this light, the twenty-first century holds very real challenges for those of us who are living in it. And it is precisely those challenges that demand a creative response in our asynchronous world.

A Cyclical History

What can we say about life in the twenty-first century, both thus far as well as in the decades to come? Alongside Pinker's convincing argument that human society writ large has become progressively less violent, there is compelling evidence that ours is a discontented and disoriented age. In *Flow*, psychologist Csikszentmihalyi provides a counterweight to Pinker's statistics:

> The three- to fourfold increase in social pathology over the last generation holds true in an astonishing number of areas. For instance, in 1955 there were 1,700,000 instances of clinical intervention involving mental patients across the country; by 1975 the number had climbed to 6,400,000. Perhaps not coincidentally, similar figures illustrate the increase in our national paranoia: during the decade from 1975 to 1985 the budget authorized to the Department of Defense climbed from $87.9 billion a year to $284.7 billion—more than a threefold increase [the 2018 budget is projected at $639.1 billion]. (15)

Like Pinker, Csikszentmihalyi goes on to list a wide variety of more subtle statistics to support his thesis that contemporary life— even in successful, developed countries—is fundamentally dissatisfying and even chaotic.

Can both Pinker and Csikszentmihalyi be right? Can contemporary life be both improved (less violent) and yet fearful (more paranoid)? The answer is demonstrably *yes*. As Csikszentmihalyi himself writes, "despite having achieved previously undreamed-of miracles of progress, we seem more helpless in facing life than our less privileged ancestors" (15–16).

The answer, I believe, lies in the third view of human history— neither optimistic nor pessimistic but cyclical. In his 1989 book, *The Culture We Deserve*, Jacques Barzun describes how "entire civilizations do perish." In his last chapter, titled "Toward the Twenty-First

Century," Barzun compares our own time to previous periods of decadence:

> The tremendous endings of Greece and Rome are not a myth. True, life somehow continues after the fall, but it is that very "somehow" which tells us that something above mere existence has disappeared. That something is what we call civilization. It is an expression of collective life cast in determinate ways, an expression that includes power, "growth," a joyous or grim self-confidence, and other obvious signs of a going concern. But it consists also of tacit individual faith in certain ideals and ways of life, seconded by a general faith in the rightness of the scheme. It follows that widespread disbelief in those intangibles, and the habits they produce in day-to-day existence, brings on the dissolution of the whole. (162–63)

Normally, we are protected by what Csikszentmihalyi labels the "shields" against discontent: "religion, patriotism, ethnic traditions, and habits instilled by social custom" (12). Barzun explores why these shields (even science) no longer hold at the end of an epoch—they have never held thus—and why despair and indifference can be the result even in the midst of plenty.

Such, then, is the twenty-first century: a time when the old social and cultural order has dissolved and has yet to be replaced with a new. Physical violence may have declined, and yet psychological doubt and personal despair have risen as we wait for a new cultural and/or economic order to declare itself. And finally, the whole historical process is exacerbated by the fall of national and social borders due to rampant economic and technological revolution.

Given all of this volatility, what can we say with any certainty about life in 2050?

INEVITABLE GLOBALIZATION

We may safely say that life in 2050 will be *global* in spirit rather than regional or national. The forces that shape the quality of our lives—especially financial forces—will be determined by the international marketplace and the global economy. In *The World Is Flat*, Thomas Friedman argues that nations will no longer have as much power as large, international companies, which are less interested in local concerns or even national politics than they are in international trends and global issues. Recent retrograde movements in American and European politics to the contrary, the world is growing smaller, and borders—all borders—are becoming more porous in a way that no wall can ever block.

Not only is this globalization driven by financial forces more powerful than any governmental edict, but it is also galvanized by factors as diverse as the global migrations of refugees and exiles, dissolving political identity and national boundaries, international awareness of what were once local issues, and . . . technology. Every message of significance in the twenty-first century—for better or worse—moves at the speed of light: money transfers, medical records, personal information, diatribes of hate and poems of love, images as well as words on email, Twitter, Instagram, and Snapchat. You now have a plethora of media with which to communicate with your friends (or your enemies) in Sweden or South Africa or India. In this brave new world of instantaneous communication, national identity has almost ceased to matter despite the drum-pounding efforts of politicians everywhere.

How have the newer generations responded? With international love affairs and marriages, with mixed race and ethnicity, with a more fluid definition of gender, with shaved heads and vibrant hair, with a kind of determined willingness to be at home almost anywhere. In a recent *New York Times* editorial (February 16, 2018), David Brooks described this new "social type [as] the Amphibians—people who can thrive in radically different environments." Brooks writes:

> The Amphibians are pluralism personified. Pluralism, remember, isn't just living with difference, or tolerance. It's the weaving together of different life commitments. It's being planted here and also being planted there, but somehow forming yourself into a third thing, one coherent personality. Amphibians make E pluribus unum their life mission.

Not to put too fine a point on Brooks's elegant description, but dual citizenship is the wave of the future—if world citizenship doesn't make the notion of duality obsolete.

RAPID CHANGE

Life in 2050 will also feel even more *volatile* in terms of the rate of change. Brooks's Amphibians will be on the move, figuratively if not literally. They will be adapting to new technologies and new social constructs, new economic and political movements, new stresses and new ways of combating stress. The algebraic notion of rate of change (ROC) might be defined as the speed at which a variable changes over a specific period of time. ROC is often used when speaking about momentum, and it can generally be expressed by the slope of a line on a graph; the steeper the slope the more rapid the change. Who worries about ROC? Economists and investors track the history of a specific stock using ROC. Historians use a similar concept to study how quickly social phenomena evolve: a cultural revolution equals a high degree of algebraic momentum.

The point of introducing the concept of rate of change into this conversation is that, as I write, globalization is happening at such a high ROC that it is almost impossible to track with any sense of validity. It may well be that the only constant about life in 2050 will be change, and the rate of that change is as yet unimaginable.

A MORE COMMUNAL SOCIETY

Another characteristic of life in 2050 is that it will quite probably be *communal*. By this, I mean that new forms of community will surely evolve, in which the more or less traditional family will change into new and unexpected shapes and sizes. Our own version of the blended family—which includes multiple generations and close step-relations—is the preview of what is to come. Add the increasing fluidity in both gender identity and sexual preference (two entirely different things), as well as the numbers of children who will be orphaned or otherwise abandoned in an increasingly chaotic world, and you begin to see in how many different ways the puzzle pieces of family might be assembled—and reassembled—in the decades to come. It's already apparent that some forms of community (and thus communication and communion) will be virtual rather than actual—characterized by URLs rather than street addresses. In other words, we will redefine terms like *tribe* and *clan* and even *community* itself in our efforts to find new and different ways of satisfying our need for communion.

LONGEVITY

Finally, twenty-first-century life in the developed countries of the globe has the potential of becoming increasingly *long*. Length of life is a characteristic of twenty-first-century existence that is often discussed in terms of an aging population, the graying of society. But there are other factors involved in long life besides health care and retirement benefits. As life itself stretches out, so does the length of one's career, one's varied family ties, one's education. Rather, I should have written *careers, families,* and *ongoing education*—plural.

How Will Longevity Affect Careers?

According to the most recent numbers from the Bureau of Labor Statistics (2015), the average worker currently holds ten different jobs before age 40, and this number is projected to grow. Forrester Research predicts that today's youngest workers will hold 12 to 15 jobs in their lifetimes. Furthermore, this trend is even more systemic than this first glance might suggest. According to most common career statistics, the average person will change *careers* five to seven times during his or her working life. And as that working life gets longer and the rate of change faster, the average individual in a developed country will change careers somewhere in the neighborhood of ten times over a 40- or 50-year span. The idea of entering a job in your twenties and moving inexorably up the ladder with the same employer and retiring to the country after 30 years is as outdated as your father's white shirt and narrow black tie. Organization man has already become organization nomad (woman *or* man) simply because the organizations themselves will come and go during the long run of your working life, and the various jobs within organizations are constantly changing and moving geographically. Friedman has already documented much of this in *The World Is Flat*, and now, 13 years later, the world is growing flatter as jobs shift shape and skitter across national boundaries.

How Will Longevity Affect Families?

In addition to a much longer and more fluid working experience, successful women and men will likely experience a greater variety of living situations. They will likely have multiple marriages and live in a variety of places, quite probably in more than one country (this is already true in Europe where countries are smaller and closer together). They will speak more languages at home as well as at work. They will become important figures in the lives of their partner's biological children as well as their own. In other words, longer lives mean exposure to more and different experiences, in both personal as well as public life.

How Will Longevity Affect Education?

One final attribute of longer life in developed countries is the desire and need for ongoing education. The lives of successful women and men were once characterized by one advanced degree earned in your twenties, which then translated into a career more or less specialized and more or less consistent. As our lives lengthen—especially our working lives—the need for continuous education of one kind or another will become the norm for many successful people. Much of this education will be what might be termed informal rather than formal: apprenticeship to a craftsperson, working in a nonprofit, training for a marathon, taking community college classes, reading and studying a difficult subject on your own or with a few others, and so on. But if you pause and look around, the preponderance of book clubs and study groups, "middle-aged" women and men "taking classes" and traveling, and—perhaps most telling of all—postcareer women and men enrolling in special colleges for creative retirement are all steadily growing in affluent societies.

What can we say about life in 2050? Certainly, we can't predict what your job or your daughter's job will be—or even what jobs will be most prevalent or rewarding—simply because many of those jobs don't exist yet. The social realities are even more unpredictable. To quote William Butler Yeats, 2050 may well be a world in which "the ceremony of innocence is drowned; the best lack all conviction, while the worst are full of passionate intensity."

And yet, based on current trends viewed in the context of the long record of human history, there are things we can predict about life 30 years hence. Your life, and your children's lives, will be global, volatile, communal, and last longer than you might ever expect.

In that world . . . who among us will thrive?

CHAPTER 5

THE CREATIVE
PERSONALITY

In *The Lessons of History*, Will and Ariel Durant define civilization as "social order promoting cultural creation." It seems like a fair enough definition, especially if you accept the notion that there are multiple civilizations and that they rise and fall.

Given that our quest is to define personal success in 2050, might we reframe our question using the Durants' definition? Might we ask whether an age of social *disorder* promotes *individual* creation? And if so, in whom?

My reply is that social disorder is often the incubator for creative individuals, women and men who are symphonic, ambitious, marginal, resilient, productive—in short, people who bounce when thrown down and are most at home in unpredictable, even erratic circumstances. On the last page of *The Culture We Deserve*, Jacques Barzun writes that "what is wanted is an open conspiracy of genuine Young Turks who will turn their backs on analysis and criticism and reinvent" themselves and their culture (183). But Barzun is concerned not so much with the individual but with the society at large, a collective awareness and rebirth rather than a personal route to success. If we ask ourselves who will become these Young Turks, then we are back to the definition of *creative* rather than the tired litany of *smart*.

We have already said that our Young Turks (who might be any age from 20 to 80) will eschew "analysis and criticism" in order to make their own way. David Brooks offers a further clue when he writes that his Amphibians (whom he sincerely hopes will become Young Turks) "have that on the edge-of-inside mind-set. They are within the circle of the group, but at the edge, where they can most easily communicate with those on the outside. They are at the meeting-place of difference where creativity happens." Creativity again, and with an echo of Howard Gardner's notion that creators thrive in a state of "marginality."

SYMPHONIC INTELLIGENCE

One way of interpreting Brooks's notion of the Amphibian is to revisit Gardner's groundbreaking theory of multiple intelligences and to remind ourselves that Gardner's own study of creativity revealed individuals who were a blend of multiple intelligences rather than masters of one. As individuals, they were each the human meeting place of different intelligences.

All of this suggests that blended intelligences—and the careers that accompany them—will serve you well in the decades to come. First, two or three intelligences working in harmony provide insight and power far beyond that of a single specialization. Second, when life in a fractured world closes off one area of pursuit (occupation, expression, exploration, etc.), there will be others of equal or greater attraction that a creative individual can take advantage of.

If our fragmented twenty-first-century world is characterized by transience and unpredictability, then the only proper response is a kind of supple resilience made up of many intellectual fibers.

We don't have a handy, modern term for an individual who has the fully developed multiple intelligences described here. *Renaissance man or woman, polymath, jack-of-all-trades*—all seem dated and not quite up to the task of describing someone who faces a mercurial world with multiple skill sets. Furthermore, we don't have a good term for the individuals who merge their multiple intelligences in new and adaptive ways.

I would propose the phrase *symphonic intelligence* for an especially adept blend of cognitive talents. To name the individual who possesses symphonic intelligence, I would suggest *sage*. Thus, we have the complementary terms *sagacity* and *sagacious*. A sage is someone who has through experience—success followed by failure followed by success—attained mastery. Both of these terms, *symphonic intelligence* and *sage*, stand in stark contrast to the notion of prodigy that our current society is so enamored of. A prodigy is someone who exhibits surprising skill in a single intelligence early in life, thereby producing prodigious success without failure. A sage is all the more remarkable because she or he reaches a tougher and more sophisticated blend of intelligences by constantly adapting to an uncertain and fickle world—a world defined by failure as well as success.

THE COMPANY MAN

In a stable society like the one that existed in the United States and some parts of Europe following World War II, there was a strong sense of cultural purpose and social predictability—at least for privileged segments of the population. Success in school opened the door to a college diploma and perhaps a graduate or professional degree beyond that. It was a world in which specialization—particularly in law or medicine or finance—led naturally to prestige and wealth. The highest goal was to become a millionaire or the equivalent in other countries and currencies. True, it was a world dominated by what came to be known as WASPs (white Anglo-Saxon Protestants) and only male WASPs at that, but in 1950, we hadn't yet challenged the notion of male supremacy.

Once an ambitious young man of that era left college and entered the work world, his path was defined by the company. In

The Organization Man (1956), William H. Whyte studied how dedication to life within large corporations led to a dependence on the
group to define progress and define the lives of individuals. One
of Whyte's central themes is that average Americans in the postwar years subscribed to a collectivist ethic rather than the myth
of rugged individualism. After the war, as the American economy
exploded, many middle- and upper-class Americans became con-
vinced that organizations and groups could make better decisions
than individuals, so that service to your employer—to the organization—became logically preferable to advancing one's individual
creativity or lifestyle. Whyte himself was a critic; he believed that
the creative individual could produce better outcomes than collective processes and groupthink. He argued that our devotion to the
organizations that shaped American life led to risk-averse executives
who could move slowly and steadily up the corporate ladder and
expect jobs for life as long as they made no outrageous mistakes.
Most middle-class, white Americans saw this as a path with little risk
but high reward.

It is no accident that in the 50 years following World War II
our idea of intelligence as a static, measurable capacity (an individual's IQ) grew up in the shadow of a society dedicated to order
and predictability. Large organizations required workers and especially bosses who were "smart" as well as loyal. What they did not
want was workers who were creative and individualistic. In other
words, our definition of intelligence resonated with our ideas about
success and duty. All were terms that meant something within a
narrow, predictable worldview where good behavior and the Prot-
estant work ethic were consistently rewarded. As our worldview
becomes more complex and less certain (see the previous chapter), the meaning of these words began to shift as well. Indeed, the
notion of IQ as a static and determining factor in an individual's

fate has all but lost its meaning, even though we occasionally still use the term as if it were 1950.

Whyte's book is a sociological classic. It serves both as a warning of what can happen when a society becomes too complacent and as a stark counterpoint to the developed world a century later—our target year of 2050. The organizations themselves have changed radically, and many have come and gone. The executives who now walk the halls and haunt the boardrooms of large businesses are a much more diverse group; it's not just the shirts that are no longer white. Were the author alive today, he might be tempted to title a subsequent study *The Organization Woman*. And although these shifts in race, ethnicity, and gender are vitally important, what is even more fundamental is the rise of individual creativity as the new smart. And as we're beginning to understand, there is no creativity without risk.

The last chapter laid out the case that life in 2050 will be global, volatile, communal, and long. Let's consider each in turn as a lens through which to view creativity.

GLOBAL CREATIVITY

Globalization immediately suggests the need for successful people to travel comfortably in other countries and cultures. It suggests the need for a facility with languages or at least the willingness to navigate reality with alternate language speakers. The world may also come to you rather than demanding that you come to it. It means that successful individuals will work comfortably in what we term "foreign" locales and environments and welcome those we now call "aliens" onto their home turf. It means that when a job or a relationship migrates, successful women and men will at least consider following the commitment beyond the horizon. As David Brooks termed it, "it's being planted here and also being planted there, but somehow forming yourself into a third thing, one coherent personality" regardless of where you're planted.

Ten years ago, I assumed that by 2050 dual citizenship would be common. Now, I wonder if there won't be an übercitizenship, a person of many countries. Indeed, many successful people already lead multinational lives. This phenomenon can only become more common among those who value economic success as indicative of personal value, because the economy will force ambitious people to become international in their focus. One will have to be much nimbler to follow the money.

VOLATILE CREATIVITY

We also described our century as increasingly volatile; the rate of change is increasing. Most successful people in this age of acceleration will be fully self-aware. In a real sense, they will know who they are and are not, and so can keep their poise in a fluid world. They will pick and choose the technologies that fit their own style and purpose rather than falling prey to every breakthrough. They will make existential choices about all matter of personal and professional questions without merely conforming to the prevailing fads or kowtowing to the organization. They will seek out their own truths and become fluent at expressing those truths, both in action and in word. Conformity will no longer be a rewarding path in 2050 because the group mentality will be too distorted and too transient. Creative individuals will have to remain faithful to who they are at their core to navigate constantly shifting external realities. Ironically, they will have to cultivate an internal stillness to move quickly and decisively through the external world. Thus, the second implication for life in an increasingly volatile world is the paramount need for resilience.

COMMUNAL CREATIVITY

Communal life will also be much more transient in 2050. By communal, I mean *where* successful people will live and *with whom*. Previously, I might have used the term *family life*, but that suggests that some form of biological family still rules the literal and figurative roost. The idea of marriage itself still seems in play, as most developed countries in the West have legalized marriage for same-sex couples, but the idea of a single, lifelong, monogamous relationship no longer seems especially feasible. This is true, in part, because we are living and working longer; more and more women are earning their own livelihoods, thus freeing them of economic dependency; and we will all change jobs and physical locations with increasing frequency. The idea of an extended family will take on new meaning in an increasingly complex world: Your family will include various step- as well as biological relatives; it will include a variety of transgender individuals as well as multiracial and multinational relationships; and it will be extended over geographical distances as well as generations. It will require empathy, acceptance, and tender, loving care to maintain.

If this brief sketch of a communal family circa 2050 seems far-fetched, look around you. This sort of extended and complex community life has always been characteristic of creative people, even those creators (like the frigid Eliot and Freud, or the sadistic Picasso) who are interpersonal failures. Furthermore, an extended, complex, even fluid family life is becoming increasingly common in most if not all developed countries. We have met the future of family and community, and the future is now. To borrow the title of a contemporary television drama, *this is us*. What is required of *us* by this sort of convoluted and mercurial communal life is openness and creativity combined with a willingness to forgive and to accept.

THE TEN-YEAR RULE

In his 1651 book *Leviathan,* English political philosopher Thomas Hobbes famously described life outside a well-structured society as "solitary, poor, *nasty, brutish, and short.*" It's with no little irony, then, that we're describing a similarly unstructured life 400 years later as global, volatile, communal, and *long.* Life expectancy matters because success will mean a longer narrative containing both tragedy and comedy, losing as well as winning—reshaping and redefining one's life over many decades. In terms of the creativity required to succeed in such a life, Gardner's "ten-year rule" comes to mind, "in which important events and breakthroughs occurred at approximately ten-year intervals. . . . As has already been well documented in studies of cognitive psychology, it takes about ten years for an individual to gain initial mastery of a domain." This rule, or something like it, may well apply to careers, homes, and personal relationships as well as more traditional creative endeavors. In other words, a life history of 90 or 100 years might well be graphed in successive waves rather than straight lines and the story told in distinct chapters rather than one continuous and homogeneous plotline. Those who thrive will sense opportunity where others see failure, and they will be gifted at redefinition and rebirth.

Life in 2050 will be different from other historical periods of unrest and decadence—in scale if not in kind. It will be a profoundly existential age, in which the value of our lives and our actions will be ambiguous at best. Those who thrive will invest that world with their own significance and not accept the roles and definitions assigned to them by a prevailing ideology. These creators will find ways to define the group rather than being defined by the group.

They will manufacture meaning out of the shifting materials they are given to work with as they move nimbly from one setting to another. Because they see the world around them through multiple lenses (not one specialization) and approach that world through various intelligences, they will be able to merge and meld various insights into a more sophisticated response than they would ever have been allowed in previous generations. They won't conform; they will reform.

CHAPTER 6

DYNAMIC AND LIFELONG

In our fast-paced, technology-obsessed society, we often fall prey to the illusion of youthful success. As a result, Silicon Valley entrepreneurs wonder if they're washed up at 30, and intellectual prodigies fear the decrepitude of middle age. Indeed, if life consists of a race to fame or prosperity, then a fast start and an early sprint seem like essential components, and if you don't win early, you might not win at all.

The reality is that in the twenty-first century, the sprint has been replaced by the marathon. Because the path to good fortune is, in our world, so volatile and complex, the need for speed has been replaced by the need for agility and staying power. In short, those who will thrive in this world are those who are productive in a variety of ways over the long journey of life.

SOLON AND CROESUS

In what is generally considered to be the earliest history written in the West (from the fifth century BC), the Greek Herodotus recounts the story of a confrontation between the Athenian philosopher and statesman Solon and the Lydian king Croesus. According to Herodotus, Solon traveled on an extended world tour after crafting the Athenian Constitution early in the sixth century BC. When the philosopher arrived in the court of the fabulously rich and powerful

Croesus, he was lodged at the royal palace. After several days, the king "bade his servants conduct Solon over his treasuries, and show him all their greatness and magnificence." After this lavish display, Croesus asks Solon to tell him who is the happiest man the Athenian has met during his travels.

Solon answers readily, first by nominating Tellus of Athens, a man who lived a long and happy life in the bosom of his extended family and then was fortunate enough to die in battle defending his countrymen. Croesus is taken aback by this answer—which is honest but not flattering—and goes on to ask who is the second happiest individual Solon has encountered, fully expecting to be given second place. Solon again frustrates the king by naming the Argive twins Cleobis and Bito, famous athletes who honored both the gods and their mother through legendary feats of strength and devotion. As a result, the gods allowed them to die peacefully while asleep in the temple after consuming a celebratory feast. "When Solon had thus assigned these youths the second place, Croesus broke in angrily, 'What, stranger of Athens, is my happiness, then, so utterly set at nought by thee, that thou dost not even put me on a level with private men?'"

At this point in the narrative, let us join Herodotus (as translated by George Rawlinson):

> "Oh! Croesus," replied the other, "thou askedst a question concerning the condition of man, of one who knows that the power above us is full of jealousy, and fond of troubling our lot. A long life gives one to witness much, and experience much oneself, that one would not choose. Seventy years I regard as the limit of the life of man. . . . The whole number of the days contained in the seventy years will thus be twenty-six thousand two hundred and fifty, whereof not

one but will produce events unlike the rest. Hence man is wholly accident. For thyself, oh! Croesus, I see that thou art wonderfully rich, and art the lord of many nations; but with respect to that whereon thou questionest me, I have no answer to give, until I hear that thou hast closed thy life happily." (7)

We might profitably regard the story of Croesus and Solon as a parable about success, especially success in an uncertain world. After all, "a long life gives one to witness much, and experience much oneself, that one would not choose." Our children may reasonably expect to see 90 years or, using Solon's calculations, 33,750 days, "whereof not one but will produce events unlike the rest."

We can read the lessons inherent to this parable by simply substituting the word *successful* for *happy*. In other words, a long life yields many unforeseen challenges as well as undeserved rewards. It is how one responds to these vicissitudes that defines her or his success as well as happiness. Solon warns Croesus that it is better to be lucky than rich, for wealth, while attractive, is no shield against loss or despair:

"The wealthy man is better able to content his desires, and to bear up against a sudden buffet of calamity. The other has less ability to withstand these evils (from which, however, his good luck keeps him clear), but he enjoys all these following blessings: he is whole of limb, a stranger to disease, free from misfortune, happy in his children, and comely to look upon. . . . But in every matter it behoves us to mark well the end: for oftentimes God gives men a gleam of happiness, and then plunges them into ruin." (7–8)

It is well to remember the context of this famous exchange between Croesus and Solon, the embodiments of power versus wisdom. Solon had just left Athens after laboring to produce a democratic constitution, a government by law designed to keep at bay the decadence and violent partisanship of his own age (his own twenty-first century). He is the archetype of one who speaks truth to power regardless of the consequences.

What, then, does he mean when he tells Croesus the following?

> "He who possesses great store of riches is no nearer happiness than he who has what suffices for his daily needs, unless it so hap that luck attend upon him, and so he continue in the enjoyment of all his good things to the end of his life. For many of the wealthiest men have been unfavoured of fortune, and many whose means were moderate have had excellent luck." (7)

In the context of our own explorations, it means that none of what we currently label *riches*—high test scores and good grades, a technical degree from the best university, a choice career path, a home in the select part of town—is a guarantee of ongoing success or happiness. During a long life in a volatile world, the value of these things will wax and wane.

Furthermore, what does Solon mean when he tells us, along with Croesus, that luck trumps power or wealth? At first glance, it is tempting to read this parable as nothing more than a dire warning. It seems that what most scholars translate as *luck* is beyond our control, and therefore we are all helpless to manage the accidents of life. But if we dig deeper into the lives of the individuals whom Solon deems happy, something interesting emerges. Tellus, Cleobis, and Bito all responded to what might well have been disastrous

circumstances with Oliver Sacks's "boldness, confidence, independence of mind." After a life of undeniable privilege, it was the end
of Tellus's life that "was surpassingly glorious. In a battle between
the Athenians and their neighbours near Eleusis, he came to the
assistance of his countrymen, routed the foe, and died upon the
field most gallantly." In short, it wasn't Tellus's privileged existence that was remarkable but his willingness to leave that settled
path for the chaos of battle. Of Cleobis and Bito, Solon recounts
this tale:

> There was a great festival in honour of the goddess Juno
> at Argos, to which their mother must needs be taken in a
> car. Now the oxen did not come home from the field in
> time: so the youths, fearful of being too late, put the yoke
> on their own necks, and themselves drew the car in which
> their mother rode. Five and forty furlongs did they draw
> her, and stopped before the temple. This deed of theirs was
> witnessed by the whole assembly of worshippers. (7)

The gods were so impressed by their heroic—and creative—
response to this emergency that they were rewarded with peaceful
deaths followed by immediate fame. Regardless of how we might
view falling asleep in the temple after a banquet in your honor, for
the Greeks this was a storybook ending.

In both cases, that of Tellus and the twins, individuals of some
wealth and accomplishment are suddenly faced with dire straits
and respond with audacity. In both cases, it is not their affluence
that defines their lives but rather their creative response when that
affluence evaporates. Herodotus was writing more than 2,000 years
before Freud, but there is a psychological profile lurking in his portrait of these "happy" individuals. Tellus, Cleobis, and Bito thrive at

ᴜᴇ precise moment when their formerly settled and prosperous lives fall apart. Furthermore, it is the sum of their lives that matters, not the ephemeral markers of wealth or prestige.

Translated into modern terms, this parable suggests that those who will thrive (Solon's *happiness*) in our own divisive and unpredictable age are those who are continuously creative over a long life of challenge and growth. What matters most is an ever-present willingness to learn and adapt; as Einstein famously termed it: "Intellectual growth should commence at birth and cease only at death."

If you conform to a conventional definition of success, you will only suffer when that definition no longer holds and things fall apart, but if you create your own independent definition, you can maintain your energy and passion even into old age.

INDEPENDENT STUDY

A lifetime defined by continuous learning and cyclical growth reminds us of Howard Gardner's discovery that creativity occurs in ten-year intervals, producing significant works in surprisingly predictable patterns. In *Creating Minds*, Gardner argues that in a creative person's life a "decade of apprenticeship heightens the likelihood of a major breakthrough. Such a breakthrough generally follows a series of tentative steps, but when it occurs, it represents a decisive break from the past" (370).

Often, as Walter Isaacson has noticed about da Vinci and Benjamin Franklin, the creative mind is largely self-taught. After an initial period of apprenticeship (if apprenticeship is even available), typical creators become absorbed with independent studies of their own choosing, and their work is all the more innovative because it doesn't depend on received truths. Furthermore, those studies rarely cease with formal education or even late in life with some sort of retirement. Gardner found that his subjects "were each productive every day," always in pursuit of further understanding and expression. He notes that "Gandhi's literary output fills ninety volumes" and "Einstein worked on questions of physics until the last years of his life" (372). Part of the reason for the longevity of the creative life is that it is self-determined rather than externally motivated.

In 2014, the celebrated American author Elizabeth Spencer published a book of short stories titled *Starting Over*. Spencer is the author of nine novels, eight collections of stories, a memoir (*Landscapes of the Heart*, 1997), and a play (*For Lease or Sale*, 1989). At first glance, there's nothing particularly remarkable about such a prolific writer coming out with a new collection of stories. What is remarkable is that Spencer was born in 1921. She was 92 years old when *Starting Over* appeared, and the stories collected therein were written when she was in her mid to late eighties. And as Malcolm Jones noted in his *New York Times* review, at least one of the stories (I would argue several) "might have been written by Hawthorne or Cheever—a work of genius, in other words."

In short, these stories are not in any sense the insignificant, late work of a writer in the twilight of her career; rather, they are the product of a fully developed and fully functional creative imagination. Jones ended his review by noting that "Elizabeth Spencer seems to have spent her life watching, observing, always paying close attention, and for her it's the whole truth or nothing. As far as I can tell, she never missed a thing. Judging from the stories in her latest collection, she's not about to start now."

Imagine the audacity to have at age 92 the attitude that one is "starting over" and offering as evidence a collection of stories whose common theme is the creation of something new out of past trauma and something known out of mystery. This is the work of a sage who has earned her voice and uses it with the accumulated wisdom of decades.

Elizabeth Spencer published her debut novel, *Fire in the Morning*, in 1948 when she was only 27 years old. She was widely praised for her first three novels in turn because they were all set in her native Mississippi, and she seemed destined to become a celebrated Southern woman author, receiving that mantle from her friend Eudora Welty. Her third novel, *The Voice at the Back Door*, came within a whisper of winning the 1957 Pulitzer Prize; the jury selected it, but the more conservative board refused to make the award because *The Voice at the Back Door* was a candid report from the Deep South about civil rights.

From that point, Spencer's career took a sudden turn. The novels that followed, plus many of the stories, were set outside the South, often in Italy and Canada, countries that Spencer came to know and love. And not only did Spencer step outside the original role assigned to her as a somewhat genteel, predictably Southern woman writer, but also these new works were experimental in structure, tone, and style. They often dealt with the darker sides of the human psyche, especially the female psyche. And while Spencer did occasionally set a new work in the South, even these novels and stories were darker and more experimental, proving difficult fare for critics and scholars to digest.

It was not until the 1981 publication of *The Stories of Elizabeth Spencer* that she returned to critical favor, almost as if a bombshell exploded on the literary scene. Suddenly, fellow writers and critics were praising Spencer's mastery of the form, which in turn precipitated a long overdue reassessment of her novels. Having been in critical favor, distinctly out of favor, and then in favor once again, Spencer went on with her writing life, largely undisturbed by the extent to which her work was understood or appreciated.

Through many, varied seasons, living in both Europe and in Canada before returning to the US, Spencer continued to produce masterful fiction right up to and through her eighties—proving that creativity knows no age and does not require an adoring audience. Although it is worth saying that critical understanding did eventually catch up with Spencer's creative pace; in her seventies and eighties, she received critical recognition as well as artistic satisfaction.

Using Elizabeth Spencer as an exemplar for the creative life in full, it's worth a glance back at Gardner's expansive research into his pantheon of creative personalities. Gardner's seven prototypical creators were productive throughout the middle years of their lives and often into what we callously term old age. Gardner even noted a kind of wave pattern where the peaks of the wave represent import-ant breakthroughs, followed by periods of renewed apprenticeship and practice—often in the social or cultural margins—which lead in turn to new and different breakthroughs. As I write this, dancer and choreographer Twyla Tharp is staging a two-part homage to her early, experimental work at the Joyce Theater in New York; Tharp, who is still astonishingly productive, is 77. At the same time, composer György Kurtág is staging his long-awaited opera based on Samuel Beckett's play *Endgame* at the Teatro alla Scala in Milan; Kurtág, who was born and lives in Hungary, is 92. In these, as in so many other instances, old age, even advanced old age, brings heightened success after the challenges of early and midlife. In the case of Elizabeth Spencer, midcareer "failures" only led to new and different novels and stories.

The important point here is that the creative life is just that—a life. It's not bound by the traditional notions of an occupation or a career, from which one escapes on a regular basis and retires at the appropriate age. Rather, it is a function of one's rich inner life con-tinuing to express itself for as long as the body will allow.

When Solon tells the fabulously rich autocrat Croesus that it is impossible to tell if he is a happy man, Solon is sending a carefully coded message. To understand and weigh the extent of an individual's happiness—or wealth or success—it is necessary to place in the balance the entirety of that person's life.

In the same sense, it is necessary to consider the sum of a person's creative output over the many decades of life to evaluate her creativity. Neither wealth nor acclaim have much to do with value because both are fleeting, especially so in the volatile world of the twenty-first century.

Seen in this way, a creative life has two kinds of bandwidth: length and depth. The creative individuals who build a life out of their own unique gifts will draw on the depths of their personalities to continue producing important work despite the vagaries of social and cultural taste or the uncertainty of income. Because their motivation and sense of quality are internally generated, they can continue to be productive into the very last stages of life.

In *The Great Conversation*, Robert Maynard Hutchins argues that "what is here proposed is interminable liberal education" (52). Leaving aside for the moment what he means by "liberal education" (more on that later), Hutchins states the case for the lifelong endeavor to become educated that is typical of the creative personality. "He cannot expect to store up an education in childhood that will last all his life. What he can do in youth is to acquire the disciplines and habits that will make it possible for him to continue to educate himself all his life." It is easy to hear the echoes of Gardner's and Isaacson's creators in Hutchins's emphasis on the apprenticeship of youth followed by continuous self-education over many decades. As Hutchins argues, the creator "must use his mind; he must feel that he is doing something that will develop his highest powers and contribute to the development of his fellow men, or he will cease to be" (53).

Hutchins was writing about his ideal of the fully and liberally educated individual. He and the editors of the Great Books intended

their call for "interminable liberal education" as a universal prescription, but even Hutchins had to admit that for many people, this
is a fantasy. The majority of twenty-first-century citizens are poor
liberal artists at best. But his description does fit everything we know
about the lifelong endeavors of creative people, who are seldom sat-
isfied with the status quo and seek out the peak experiences that
come with further knowledge, deeper insight, and more profound
expression.

In his description of lifelong learning in *Flow*, Mihaly Csikszentmihalyi compares the depressing effects of "extrinsically motivated
education" in school to the thrills of intrinsically motivated learning that can come later in life. "At that point the goal of studying
is no longer to make the grade, earn a diploma, and find a good
job. Rather, it is to understand what is happening around one, to
develop a personally meaningful sense of what one's experience
is all about. From that will come the profound joy of the thinker"
(142). Writing 40 years after Hutchins and from a psychological perspective, Csikszentmihalyi echoes his call for lifelong, intrinsically
motivated learning as the key to human fulfillment.

Certainly, it is one of the keys to creativity.

CHAPTER 7

SUPPLE AND RESILIENT

Let's suppose for a moment that you're a freshman in college, 18 years old, and just beginning to address the challenges that await you both now, on campus, and when they finally kick you out into the real world. In 2050, you will be . . . well, 50—and in the middle of your century-long life.

By then, you will have lived on several continents and in multiple countries. You will have quit more than one job and been let go from several others. You will have begun and perhaps ended several primary relationships. You will have faced numerous and largely unexpected challenges in both your personal as well as your professional life. Your family will look nothing like the nuclear families from days gone by. Your own children—biological or otherwise—will have grown up in a capricious and fickle world that you probably don't understand. You and your children may have been relatively poor, even hungry at times; new research suggests that millennials in developed countries will struggle to match their parents' income. Your virtual presence (whatever it consists of in 2050) may be more salient and more socially active than your physical presence. Your adult life will have had three or four major chapters by then, and you will have barely reached what used to be called "middle age." The term *retirement* is rarely in use, and what we formerly meant by the word is not on the horizon.

In most important respects, the graph of your life will look like a saw blade:

Rather than a smooth and upwardly mobile curve:

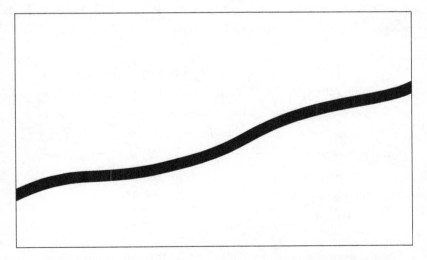

However we describe or measure your personal goals in life—wealth, stability, happiness, fame—your progress toward those goals will look and feel like a roller coaster. As such, it will require creativity on your part, and one of the most important elements of that creativity is resilience.

NEGATIVE CAPABILITY

However you conceive of resilience—adaptability, buoyancy, grit—it has to do with the ability to respond with vigor to what most of us would view as a setback, if not an outright defeat. Because life in 2050 will be both more volatile and less certain, it will provide you with fewer opportunities to swim comfortably in the mainstream and many more opportunities to respond to failure or disappointment. As a result, you are likely to suffer periods of psychological and cognitive disequilibrium, when the assumptions by which you've lived your life no longer hold true. For many people, this sort of fundamental disorientation is crippling. For the truly creative personality, it is freeing.

In a famous letter written to his brothers in 1817, the poet John Keats described what he labeled "negative capability":

> I had not a dispute but a disquisition with Dilke, on various subjects; several things dovetailed in my mind, & at once it struck me, what quality went to form a Man of Achievement especially in literature & which Shakespeare possessed so enormously—I mean Negative Capability, that is when man is capable of being in uncertainties, Mysteries, doubts without any irritable reaching after fact & reason. (41–42)

"Not a dispute but a disquisition": Keats is describing a long, perhaps more formal conversation—a drilling down into the nature of things that surpasses mere argument or passing comment. Keats's subconscious mind seems to have been at work, as "several things dovetailed" and he was "struck" by the sudden insight.

What is ironic about this experience as Keats describes it is that he himself was modeling that openness to "uncertainties, mysteries, doubts" that he praises in the "Man of Achievement." He wasn't engaged in a debate with his friend Dilke, which is important because it means that Keats wasn't tied to a particular intellectual stance in defense of his argument; rather, his mind was free to roam "without any irritable reaching after fact and reason." His invented phrase "Negative Capability" suggests the capacity to respond happily to negative events, to a mental space full of uncertainties, mysteries, and doubts.

Keats's man—or woman—of achievement, however, doesn't merely survive the shock of disappointment or defeat but instead creates out of the chaos something larger and more sophisticated than would have otherwise been possible. Deprived of the standard answer and the accepted response, she or he constructs something more complex and more inclusive. Shakespeare is Keats's prototype for accomplishment because he refused to use his plays as a vehicle for a particular philosophy or worldview. In fact, his best plays are driven by the complexities and vagaries of the human personality, not by conventions of genre or production.

Shakespeare became universal by refusing to stop with the particular. He illustrated a creative resilience that consistently reframed complex questions in larger and larger terms, often through portraying astonishingly complex characters on stage. To circle back to Keats's Negative Capability, he worked his way through his own uncertainties, mysteries, and doubts without resorting to received fact and reason.

What Keats intuited about Shakespeare is not unlike what the psychologist Howard Gardner realized after studying his prototypical creators. They produce their best work from the personal and professional margins. They are, as Gardner came to understand, supremely "self-confident, able to deal with false starts, proud and stubborn, and reluctant to admit mistakes" (362) because they trusted their own creative instincts more than those of their critics. If we equate—as do I—what Gardner calls social or even psychological marginality with Keats's "uncertainties, mysteries, doubts," then it makes perfect sense that a truly creative individual would thrive in a landscape that others would find unpredictable or even threatening. Thus the creative personality learns to see opportunity in rejection or defeat—and perhaps even seek out uncertainty or court loss. Gardner was surprised to discover that his exemplary creator attempts to retain or heighten his or her creativity through discomfort. In a sense, this is something like creator as athlete, always pushing his or her mind and spirit into more heightened awareness and productivity through training.

LEARNING FROM FAILURE

Lest we give in to the fallacy that creativity belongs only to the fractured genius or the troubled artist, let's bring Keats and Shakespeare, Freud and Graham back down to earth. The potential for creativity lies within most of us. It need not manifest itself in a symphony or a painting. As choreographer Twyla Tharp argues, "Creativity is not just for artists. It's for businesspeople looking for a new way to close a sale; it's for engineers trying to solve a problem; it's for parents who want their children to see the world in more than one way" (7).

Contemporary examples of Negative Capability abound. As I write this, two women who are at the height of successful careers in business—Sarah Robb O'Hagan and Sara Blakely—serve as exemplars of persistence and resilience. O'Hagan is the person who was

primarily responsible for bringing Gatorade back from tl
bankruptcy before she became the president of Equinox
CEO of Flywheel Sports. But before that, she was fired from her
leadership role at Virgin Atlantic and Virgin Megastore with one
week's severance. "I lost my green card application, my visa, everything," said O'Hagan, who is originally from New Zealand. "It was
pretty devastating." She recovered to work at Atari but, after two
years, was laid off there. The lesson she took away from these experiences? "Failure is the greatest personal trainer that you will ever
have," she told CNN. Risks "can lead to embarrassing failures,"
O'Hagan argued. But "failure, once you get through it, will lead you
somewhere better."

Forbes named Sara Blakely the youngest self-made billionaire in
2012. But before Blakely invented Spanx, she failed in her ambition
to become a lawyer and bombed in her job selling fax machines
door to door. It was only when she solved the age-old problem of
what to wear under a pair of white slacks by cutting off a pair of
tights that her inherent self-confidence and willpower paid off. She
explained that she was taught that failure always precedes success:
"Growing up, my dad used to encourage my brother and me to fail,"
she said. "I didn't realize it at the time, but he was just redefining
failure for me. Failure became about not trying, not the outcome."
It is no accident that two of the most successful businesswomen in
the current world marketplace both define their success in the context of previous failures and explain that success in terms of leaning
into failure and learning through it. By definition, creativity is the
imaginative response to frustration and discouragement.

Ultimately, we all have within us the potential to respond with grace
and power to the mystery. Furthermore, we don't have to go looking

for asynchrony in order to inspire our imaginations; the twenty-first century will provide all the anxiety and doubt any of us could wish for. What we must learn to do in response is cease straining after conventional fact and reason when it no longer applies and create new questions with fresh answers.

CHAPTER 8

PRODUCTIVE

Creators make or invent things. The end results of their play or work are products or performances of value to themselves and others. And, ultimately, the quality of those products or performances is how their creativity should be measured. Furthermore, because that work is quite often unique, it cannot be either assessed or predicted by traditional means.

MEASURING INTELLIGENCE WITH STANDARDIZATION

Throughout most of the twentieth century and up to the present day, the prevalent notion of intelligence has been based on the assumption that it can be measured by a test. As Gardner summarizes it in *Creating Minds*:

> Thanks to the revolution in psychological measurement (or psychometrics), associated particularly with the work of Alfred Binet in Paris and Lewis Terman in California, the concept of "intelligence" and its putative measure "IQ" were operationalized early in the twentieth century. . . . Every individual was thought to possess a certain amount of intelligence, possibly as his or her birthright, possibly as a result of nurture; the kinds of brief verbal and numerical items that populate IQ tests were thought sufficient to indicate an individual's intelligence. (19)

The result was an explosion of various sorts of standardized tests that were intended to measure intelligence, and that attitude toward standardization is just as powerful today as it was a hundred years ago. Children are still commonly described in terms of their percentile scores against national and local norms, and far-reaching decisions about their education are made based on those scores.

This deeply ingrained devotion to the "science" of quantifying individual human potential or skill is everywhere to be seen. Wherever competition is the order of the day, some few must win and many must lose the game, even when the game is something as complex as human cognition. As a result, most institutions— including almost all educational institutions—deal in rank ordering the individuals who pass through their doors.

TESTING FOR CREATIVITY

Starting in the middle of the last century, psychologist J. P. Guilford publicly called for a concerted effort to evaluate creativity in the same way many Western cultures were already assessing intelligence. Guilford himself led the way in developing prototypes for evaluating creativity, and others soon joined the cause. There were problems. Gardner describes how the traditional notion of intelligence is both like and unlike creativity:

> The key idea in the psychologist's conception of creativity has been *divergent thinking*. By standard measures intelligent people are thought of as convergers—people who given some data or a puzzle, can figure out the current (or at any rate, the conventional) response. In contrast, when given a stimulus or a puzzle, creative people tend to come up with many different associations, at least some of which are

idiosyncratic and possibly unique. Prototypical items on a creativity test ask for as many uses as possible for a brick, a range of titles for a story, or a slew of possible interpretations of an abstract line drawing: a psychometrically creative individual can habitually issue a spectrum of divergent responses to such an item, at least some of which are rarely encountered in the responses of others. (20)

In response to Guilford's challenge, psychometricians came up with a battery of creativity tests, which led us eventually to several conclusions. First, creativity is not intelligence (meaning that a given individual may have far more of one quotient than the other); second, creativity tests are reliable (meaning that the same individual can take the same test multiple times and get similar results); and third, although reliable, *creativity tests aren't valid*. What?

Creativity Tests Do Not Predict Success

High scores on the creativity tests that became popular during the second half of the twentieth century and the first decade of the twenty-first century do not necessarily correlate with the ability to produce creative work in the test individual's vocation or avocation. Creativity tests are even less satisfactory than intelligence tests in predicting success across the broad spectrum of human activity. They don't predict which musician will become a gifted composer or performer, which young writer will become a skilled poet or novelist, which extroverted youth will become a stage presence, or which obsessive sketcher will become a remarkable painter or sculptor. Nor do they predict which strong science student will do groundbreaking research, which ambitious business student will make a fortune, or which sibling who loves to cook will become an award-winning chef.

Perhaps because of the very nature of creativity itself—it does, after all, have to do with marginality and individuality—it's difficult to measure and all but impossible to predict.

Measuring the Creation

What we can measure, however, are the results. We can judge the significance and sophistication of the concert, the novel, the performance, the painting, the research, and the portfolio. We can, if we're lucky, eat the meal prepared by the chef. For better or worse, the creative act is not predictable, and therefore the creative potential cannot be tested with foresight. Rather, it must be measured in terms of the result—in hindsight.

For this reason, most recent attempts to measure creativity—including those by Mihaly Csikszentmihalyi, the author of *Flow*—have focused not on the individual but on the work; they attempt to measure either how new and different the current work is from previous work or how valuable the work is in some larger context. For Csikszentmihalyi, the value of the creative work can be measured only within a given domain (financial investment, for example) and field (the authorities in that domain). Even this model breaks down, however, when a creator such as Machiavelli or Freud creates a new domain (political science or psychology) that precipitates a new field of study. Or when a creative genius like Steve Jobs recreates our most fundamental relationship to technology, and through technology to each other. Regardless of how the production of a creative life is measured, however, the unit of measurement is the creation, not the creator.

ENCOURAGING CREATIVITY IN EVERYONE

We are back to where we started in this chapter: Creators make or produce things—new and unusual things that exercise their imaginations and change the way we view the world. Occasionally, they produce work (or play) that is truly groundbreaking.

There are three important implications that flow from this insight. First, because the metrics of creativity are based on *production* rather than *potential,* even the most skilled psychometrician can't presort or predetermine which children have the most creative potential. In fact, as Gardner and countless others have pointed out, all children are creative in their play. Creative play itself is a significant part of the learning process in childhood, and most adult creators still retain a childlike joy in the flow of production.

Second, since we can't predict who will ultimately produce the profound poem or the life-changing political movement, we must treat all as if they possess the innate ability to create—not just in early childhood, when we still recognize the power and significance of imagination, but throughout adolescence and adulthood. Appropriately, this focus on the creativity of all resonates perfectly in the world in which we live, an asynchronous and volatile time and place. In short, a divergent world demands divergent personalities, regardless of where they come from.

Third, we must recognize and resist the fundamental urge to measure ourselves and our children by standardizing potential and rewarding test scores. Although the notions of traditional intelligence and measurable IQ might have served us well in an era of conventional values and predictable growth, they fail utterly to prepare us for life in the twenty-first century.

Those who thrive in 2050 will work comfortably from the constantly shifting margins, not sit stolidly in the middle. They will be known for what they produce, not what they scored or where they went to school. They will give the gifts of their work rather than being labeled gifted.

CHAPTER 9

A NEW FLUENCY

The *Merriam-Webster* definition of the word *fluid* begins with "particles that easily move and change their relative position without a separation of the mass and that easily yield to pressure: capable of flowing." In its derivation, the word is the first cousin of the term *fluent*, which in general usage means a distinctive ease and grace of movement or usage, often in relation to the mastery of a language. It turns out that both words descend from the same linguistic ancestors, first in Latin and then in French. Their separate but related evolution—over thousands of years—reminds us that to be fluent is to move easily and gracefully across difficult and demanding terrain. A dancer can express fluent movement, and a mathematician can be fluent in geometric transformations. If we trace the ideas expressed by *fluency* and *fluid* back to their roots, we discover they are one and the same.

The *Tao Te Ching*, the ancient Eastern classic, argues that the supreme path through life is like that of *water*. In the 78th chapter, the fabled master Lao Tzu says simply that "under the sky, nothing is softer or more yielding than water. And yet when it attacks firm, rigid things, none of them can win against it" (translation by Chad Hansen).

In roughly the same era, the Greek philosopher Heraclitus was famously quoted by Plato as saying that you could not step into the same river twice, because the water flowing past was always new. Change—both within and without—is ceaseless.

Now, 2,500 years later, a twentieth-century Hungarian émigré to the United States, the psychologist Mihaly Csikszentmihalyi, argues that based on decades of research, the peak human experience can be summed up in one word: *flow*.

CHANGE INSPIRES CREATIVITY

There exists an underlying link within these various linguistic, spiritual, and psychosocial insights that keep emerging over thousands of years of human existence. The missing conceptual bridge is that human development and human fulfillment arise not out of stasis or predictability but out of change. Although we may desire rest or stability, they do not inspire us. What is ultimately most enjoyable, most rewarding, is the imaginative response to challenge. Creativity always involves change.

One of the best examples of fluid creativity is the jazz musician. The genius of jazz is improvisation. A jazz combo may play the same piece a hundred times and never play it exactly the same way twice; on any given night, the various musicians respond not only to the nature of the music itself but also to each other as they hand the piece back and forth, creating new and intricate riffs on a well-known theme.

The role of improvisation is so central to jazz that neuroscientists have begun to study what happens to the human brain of a gifted jazz musician when she or he is playing a jazz piece versus a memorized composition. One of the first scientists—and musicians—to study this, Dr. Charles Limb, discovered several interesting phenomena. First, the section of the brain that allows us to express ourselves most fully, the medial prefrontal cortex, becomes much more active, and in a way that engages both the right and left sides of the brain. Second, the section of the brain that is responsible for self-inhibition and self-control, the dorsolateral prefrontal cortex, goes dormant.

Play something that is prescribed and memorized, and the brain is not only less engaged but also maintains its rule-following function. Play something spontaneous and free-flowing, and the brain simultaneously comes alive and tells its inhibition centers to take a nap. As Limb explains, "The brain is taking a known structure and deviating from it in intentional ways that are not pre-planned" (reported to CNN on 29 April 2018).

THE NEUROSCIENCE OF CREATION

Fortunately, jazz is not the only art form in which improv trumps script. Limb has gone on to study improvisational comedians and caricature artists. Other neuroscientists have become interested in the brain function of painters and dancers when they are in full creative motion. This new wave of neuroscience is a way of studying the essence of creativity itself because it gives us a chance to watch the creative function of the brain in real time. Watching a creator create—a painter paint, a dancer dance, a jazz musician in full riff—inspires a similar response from a sensitive mind. In other words, there is something deeply moving, even pleasurable, about being present when an artist is in full creative motion because the unpredictability of creation allows the audience an opportunity to fill in the gaps, to let the imagination leap forward into the empty spaces being filled in real time. In short, to be witness to creation is to be invited into the process—to experience it neurologically.

One of the first insights to flow out of the neuroscience of creation is that almost all human beings have a startling potential for spontaneity if they can learn to let go of their insecurities and fully engage in the moment. Creativity can be expressed in everything from gardening to interior design, from cooking meals to telling jokes, from photography to doodling in the margins of a meeting agenda. What seems to be required—at least for some kinds of creativity—is releasing inhibitions and embracing the moment.

PREPARATION PRECEDES PLAY

Is jazz the answer to the challenges of twenty-first-century life? Some students of creativity would say not. Arne Dietrich, author of *How Creativity Happens in the Brain*, posited four types of creativity with corresponding different brain activities. For Dietrich, creativity could be categorized as either deliberate (whether cognitive or emotional) or spontaneous (again, either cognitive or emotional). Those activities he would class as deliberate creativity require discipline and training—often years of training and unstinting discipline. The fluid ebb and flow of jazz or the spontaneous flashes of wit from a stand-up comedian playing with her audience doesn't sound much like careful preparation and practice leading to an eventual breakthrough. But the truth is that jazz musicians master their instruments by playing countless compositions from memory before arriving at the point when they can freely and spontaneously improvise. Stand-up comedians painstakingly write and memorize their monologues so that they can play effortlessly to their audiences. Spontaneous creativity stands firmly on the shoulders of deliberate practice and preparation. Someone who makes something look easy most often does so because of long training and careful rehearsal.

True fluency, then, comes when the artists translate careful preparation—often years of preparation—into spontaneous play. It appears effortless not because they are preternaturally gifted or possessed by spirits, but because they have invested in the work that precedes the play. Think of Picasso late in his career picking up a paint brush before a blank canvas. Think of Marie Curie in her laboratory, intuitively seeking the nature of radioactivity in pitchblende.

Think of jazz trumpeter Miles Davis riffing on a long-familiar composition in an ever-new way. But think also of a man who loves to cook, varying the ingredients in a traditional recipe that he's prepared hundreds of times just because a tiny voice inside his head suggests a new variation. Imagine an elderly woman who refuses to give up her driver's license because she has yet to drive down each of the dirt roads in her rural county.

Jazz is both the embodiment of musical spontaneity and a metaphor for the inventive instinct that lives in us all. That instinct—bold and inventive in the face of a fluid world—is the ultimate fluency.

—————

This exploration into intelligence and creativity began by arguing that the old notion of intelligence as a static quotient (and with it, the companion terms such as *clever*, *quick*, *gifted*) has ceased to mean much of value. Being *smart*, especially as it's related to test scores and school grades, has less and less to do with success in contemporary life. Both these words and the ideas they represent are worn out.

What our fragmented society requires is something different, something less static and predictable. Our new age demands something much more fluid, much more resilient—much more creative. By reframing the question of who will thrive in 2050, the following profile of successful creators was developed:

- *They will blend multiple intelligences in a way that might be described as synthetic or even symphonic.*
- *They will be ambitious and focused without being self-obsessed.*
- *They will value asynchrony and even seek it out.*
- *They will use their own marginality to generate a novel perspective and new work.*

○ *They will exhibit a steadfast resilience in all phases of life.*
○ *They will be measured by what they produce over the course of their lives, not by any static notion of capacity or quotient.*

The question now before us is how do we retrain ourselves and educate our children for a life that demands such creativity?

Part Two

SCHOOLING CREATIVITY

CHAPTER 10

THE DISCIPLINE
OF WONDER

I am by profession a public school educator. In a parallel life, I am
a novelist, which may have brought me to the topic of this book.
But I earn my daily bread by working with teachers and adminis-
trators all over the country to improve the rigor and accessibility
of their classrooms. Which means that I've spent the last 30-plus
years thinking—both consciously and unconsciously—about the
schooling that precedes a creative life.

The first and most important thing to remember is that schooling
does not equal education. Any degree, even an advanced degree,
should be understood as the commencement of the journey, not the
destination. To become educated, whether in the widest or the most
specialized sense of the term, requires a lifetime. Any one of us can
and should be better educated at 40 than at 30, at 50 than at 40, at
60 than at 50, and so on. As the philosopher Mortimer Adler wrote
in the 1980s, schooling is best understood as the preparation for
becoming educated over the course of one's lifetime, and few can be
said to *be* educated without years of thoughtful experience.

Seen through the lens of this book, we can say with even more
conviction that true creative productivity requires a lifetime. Any
one of us can and should become more imaginative and more productive as we navigate the middle decades of our lives, and on into
the sagacity of old age. For this reason, schooling, along with the

education children and adolescents receive outside school, should not finish them but open them. It should discipline their native sense of wonder and possibility rather than killing it, so that they might continue to create throughout life.

REIMAGINING EDUCATION AS INDIVIDUAL CREATIVE GROWTH

This seemingly simple realization changes the game of schooling drastically. Seen in this light, the goal is no longer to score in the highest percentile or maintain the highest grade point average. Rather, the goal is to practice the skills, create the habits, and construct the personality that equips one to continue growing and changing over decades. If students are to be judged, they must be judged based on their own individual progress and in terms of these skills and characteristics, rather than by comparing them to other students or to an external standard. Furthermore, schools themselves should be evaluated on how well they inspire such preparation for the creative life.

The second important point is that the educational community both in the United States and in many places abroad is stuck in a redundant and self-defeating cycle of preparing students for life as it was lived one, two, or even three generations ago. In her recent book on university education, Cathy N. Davidson describes this phenomenon when she argues that the schooling college and university students receive "was developed in the late nineteenth and early twentieth centuries to train farmers and shopkeepers to be factory workers and office managers. . . . Such prescriptive, disciplinary, and specialized training worked well for most of the twentieth century . . . but it makes a lot less sense for our post-industrial and post-internet world" (3). Davidson is right, of course, so far as she goes. But most of our habits and assumptions about learning are set by the time we are in college, and the battle is largely lost by that point if we have received a "modern" education in preparation for a postmodern world.

The education that needs to be reimagined and reformed begins in kindergarten and extends well beyond high school commencement. It is here that a new generation of creative individuals—our children and grandchildren—need to learn the skills and practice the habits that will render them proof against twenty-first-century fragmentation. If the first principle is that schooling is the preparation for becoming increasingly productive over a lifetime, the second is that we must deliberately school ourselves and our children for the future and not the past. This means that we must teach the characteristics of creativity starting in childhood.

A word or two of warning is apropos here: American schools and school systems have become fiercely risk-averse in the era of high-stakes accountability, and most voucher-funded options are even less flexible in face of the looming future. It may take a profound shock—such as a radical reduction in standardized testing or the vociferous demands of wise parents—to shake loose the necessary changes.

NURTURING ACTIVE REFLECTION

Since the goal is to have our schools become incubators for the creative personality rather than fold and bend that creative persona into a test-taking, rule-following organization child, where do we begin? The first step is to reimagine schools as places where we nurture the habit of reflection combined with action. Educators often bemoan the supposed anti-intellectual fervor that dominates so much of American culture; perhaps ours is not so much an anti-intellectual culture as it is anti-reflective. We value speed and volume more than meditation and judgment. Another way of saying this is that we teach facts and skills rather than conceptual understanding, based on the mistaken assumption that the concepts only get in the way of efficiency. As Hutchins wrote years ago in his ringing defense of liberal and lifelong education, the creative individual "is at home . . . in the world of practical affairs" in addition to "the world of ideas . . . because he understands the relation of the two" (4). In other words, creative people can act incisively because they are prepared to do so by study and practice. Vigorous action flows out of reflection; cogent thought flows out of potent practice. Seen through the prism of creativity as we have described it, innovative production is the result of wonder-filled activity. If there is a rhythm to creativity, it has an alternating current of action followed by reflection. Howard Gardner's research into the biographies of archetypal creators suggests the power of this pattern just as do the countless creative lives before and after his groundbreaking study.

The time has come for us to demand creative classrooms that nurture reflection and action as two complementary habits of mind and heart.

PROJECT-BASED LEARNING: CREATIVITY AS A NATURAL PROCESS

During the first decade of the century, a coalition of educators associated with the National Paideia Center developed a variation of project-based instruction that we (I was one of the designers) eventually named the Paideia Coached Project. The Coached Project is a version of unit planning for the generic classroom, regardless of age level or subject area. Our intent throughout the design process was to build on the very best that was known about human learning, both inside and outside the traditional school setting. To that end, we delved deeply into the school reform programs that were current at the time (which are not unlike most of those that are popular today). We integrated fundamental insights from the Coalition of Essential Schools, Foxfire, Understanding by Design, Problem-Based Learning, and so on. We synthesized learning theory from our own well-established tradition—the Paideia Program—by building a model that generated a complementary relationship between teaching factual recall, skill development, and conceptual understanding. More importantly, we argued that student production and performance for authentic audiences was at the very core of wise schooling.

Furthermore, we went beyond the research manufactured by schools of education and the diatribes produced by politicians to examine what the fundamental body of research into human learning told us about our species and how it develops. We dove into a seminal study on human learning published in 1993 by the American Psychological Association's Presidential Task Force on Psychology in Education titled *Learner-Centered Psychological Principles: Guidelines for School Redesign and Reform*. It's a mouthful, I admit, and in our hyper rate-of-change world, something published in 1993 may qualify as an antique if not a classic. But don't be fooled by either the title or the date. In fact, the authors drew on decades of research into the psychology of learning to develop a set of guidelines that are, in the truest sense of the term, *research-based*.

Included in these guidelines are 12 "learner-centered psychological principles" that could almost act as a guidebook for fostering creativity in our sense of the term. The first principle states:

> Learning is a natural process of pursuing personally meaningful goals, and it is active, volitional, and internally mediated; it is a process of discovering and constructing meaning from information and experience, filtered through the learner's unique perceptions, thoughts, and feelings.

The language of this first principle echoes our portrait of creativity: *active, volitional, internally mediated, discovering, constructing, unique*. What may be even more significant is that years of research argues that this kind of learning is a natural process, which in turn suggests that creativity itself is natural in human beings, rather than being a rare or force-fed phenomenon. Anthony Brandt and David Eagleman make precisely this argument in their 2017 book *The Runaway Species: How Human Creativity Remakes the World*:

> Thanks to [the human] appetite for novelty, innovation is requisite. It's not something that only a few people do. The innovative drive lives in every human brain, and the resulting war against the repetitive is what powers the colossal changes that distinguish one generation from the next, one decade from the next, one year from the next. The drive to create the new is part of our biological makeup. (32)

What's disturbing about the notion that all humans are fundamentally creative beings is that we too often lose the sense of wonder we are born with and crush it in the generations that follow—all in the name of conformity and success. But this is a sociocultural habit we can no longer afford. The creative urge not only can outlast the splendor of childhood but also will become an attribute of any healthy, evolving adult.

Personalized Schooling in a Social Environment

How do we provide schooling that honors the individual spirit while nurturing the creative "learner's unique perceptions, thoughts, and feelings"? How do we teach for the future, not the past?

The seventh principle sheds light on this dilemma:

Curiosity, creativity, and higher-order thinking are stimulated by relevant, authentic learning tasks of optimal difficulty and novelty for *each* student. (emphasis added)

Here we arrive at a profound educational paradox: *Schooling for creativity is personalized rather than standardized.* Every step we take toward
further quantification and standardization renders the work we do
in school less interesting, less inspired, and less authentic. Rather,
the learner must be allowed to "create meaningful, coherent representations of knowledge" (principle 2) "in uniquely meaningful
ways" (principle 3) rather than constantly being driven toward a
common standard or goal. Part of fostering personal creativity in
school also involves recognizing the social aspect of learning:

Learning and self-esteem are heightened when individuals
are in respectful and caring relationships with others who
see their potential, genuinely appreciate their unique talents, and accept them as individuals. (principle 10)

One theme resonates throughout these principles: critical thinking
and creativity thrive in an environment that values the individual
over the standard and allows students to work together as well as
individually.

What Are the Characteristics of Schools that Nurture Creativity?

I argued earlier that we must stop educating for the past and begin
educating for the future, and it is high time we recognize that standardization is the past and individualization is the future. In short,
the narrow convergence of intelligence is the past and the rich diver-
gence of creativity is the future.

If we glance back at the characteristics of the individual who will thrive in 2050, we see someone who blends multiple intelligences, who is ambitious and focused, who creates new work out of asynchrony and marginality, who is consistently resilient and productive. Once again, we see a twenty-first-century *profile* rather than a twenty-first-century *profession*. The question is whether we as a society have the wisdom and the will to reimagine schools as incubators for this profile.

We have learned enough about schooling over the years to describe the kind of schools and teachers that nurture this profile. But first, let's say in the strongest possible terms what a twenty-first-century school isn't. It's *not* limited to teaching and testing a narrow range of intelligences in the way that our current schools are focused almost solely on linguistic and logical-mathematical skills. It's *not* designed to teach the various subject areas in isolation, whereby students rotate through language, math, social studies, and science plus a few "related arts" or "electives" on a lockstep schedule. It's *not* built to segregate students based on perceived ability, offering the best teachers and most challenging experiences to a few students rather than to all students. It's *not* focused on a few subject areas (think "STEM") that are theoretically linked to future employability. These are old-world notions, and it's time to blow them up and start over with an eye to the future.

On the other hand, schools that nurture creativity across the broad range of human endeavor have these important characteristics:

○ They feature cross-curricular and multidisciplinary work more than subject-specific work.
○ They address the many multiple intelligences both separately and in creative blends.
○ They feature a faculty who are themselves expert in their fields, creating multiple master-and-apprentice opportunities.

○ They offer ample opportunity for students to work in teams as well as through individual performance.

○ They stress group and individual assessment that is ongoing and collaborative rather than standardized and summative.

○ They stress quality production and performance based on multiple drafts or repeated practices and rehearsals.

○ They teach the use of technology for research or production and minimize internet and social media distractions.

○ They feature learning experiences that foster resilience and focus rather than compliance and certainty.

○ They create these experiences for all students, not for a select few.

The immediate question of course is how do these characteristics translate into the reality of classroom life, whether in a completely reimagined school setting or in classrooms not too unlike those in your neighborhood school? First of all, it is only fair to say that there are schools out there that feature many of these characteristics already. Academies dedicated to teaching the arts often offer opportunities for students to do serious, cross-curricular work, thereby developing their multiple intelligences. These same schools focus on rigorous preparation for serious performance and production built on ongoing, formative assessment. And for obvious reasons, the faculty in these schools are themselves accomplished craftsmen and artists who can serve as models to their student apprentices.

Beyond this type of specialized academy dedicated to the arts, many traditional public schools have adopted various elements of project- or problem-based learning and supplemented their standard teaching with Socratic or Paideia Seminar dialogue to nurture critical and creative thinking. Few schools have achieved the rigorous blend of action and reflection that nurtures creativity, but the seeds have been planted in various communities in most first world countries.

———

In his classic 1940 volume titled *How to Read a Book*, philosopher-educator Mortimer Adler described "education: the central aim of which has always been recognized, from Socrates's day down to our own, as the freeing of the mind through the discipline of wonder." What is remarkable about this offhand statement is how it yokes together two apparent opposites: freedom and discipline. And yet that is exactly what the creative life requires—*the freeing of the mind through the discipline of wonder.*

CHAPTER 11

NURTURING
BLENDED
INTELLIGENCES

One widespread assumption that grew up in the same era as IQ is that an individual's specialization is the means to success. Parents hoped that their sons—and in later generations, their daughters—would not merely become doctors or lawyers but surgeons and trial attorneys. And beyond that lofty horizon lay an even higher plateau: they might perform heart surgery or argue before the Supreme Court. The more specialized the career, the richer the rewards and greater the status.

As a result of this pervasive paradigm, the old-fashioned notion of a liberal education, whereby a young woman or man learns to appreciate the arts and literature on the way to an enlightened life, has slowly lost its luster. As early as the 1950s, Robert Maynard Hutchins—one of the most elegant proponents of lifelong learning through the liberal arts—was arguing against the dangers of specialization as limiting the individual's ability to understand and answer the hard, existential questions facing humanity. In the postwar world, Hutchins argued that Wisdom and Judgment were being sacrificed on the altar of Income and Achievement.

STUCK IN AN OUTDATED MINDSET
THAT FOSTERS SPECIALIZATION

From a vantage point roughly 60 years later, Hutchins and others like him have lost the cultural fight. For now at least, universities across America are reluctant to label themselves liberal arts colleges or even acknowledge that the curriculum contains liberal arts requirements. Most parents who are faced with the exorbitant cost of a university education are crystal clear about the fact that they want their daughter or son to emerge with a degree that has immediate value in the marketplace. They will put up with a semester abroad, but in truth what they really want is for their children to declare a major early, leading to degrees in science, technology, or business rather than English, history, or, heaven forbid, philosophy.

This trend has trickled down into the world of K through 12 education, where one of the hottest items on most school board agendas these days is the creation of STEM (science, technology, engineering, and math) magnet schools. Middle or early college programs are being created on the campuses of local community colleges, often leading to advanced occupational study filtering down into the high school years. In almost every instance, the goal is to prepare students to work in the twenty-first century (thus the T for *technology* in STEM), primarily by having them specialize earlier and earlier in life.

The question we automatically ask is not who will that precocious 18-year-old become, but what will she do for a living?

In this way, the generalist has been replaced in our society by the specialist . . . for now. Those two words—*for now*—are significant. For as we have seen in the preceding chapters, specialization limits rather than broadens learning and potential. It intentionally fragments knowledge and understanding and eventually creates adults who are strangely lopsided in their abilities because they favor one intelligence or skill set so strongly over others. This approach to life has worked in the past—for some—but will no longer.

The Outdated Model = Bored Students

A volatile and fragmented world does not reward specialization; if anything, it punishes it. What our world rewards are integration and flexibility. By integration, I mean not just multiple intelligences but the yoking of intelligences in new and creative ways. The twenty-first century is the landscape of the mathematician-designer, the scientist-poet, the naturalist-writer, the athlete-musician, and so on. Those who are comfortable playing multiple roles and view challenges through multiple lenses will thrive while single-entity specialists will only survive.

The immediate question, then, is how do we train a generation of innovative thinkers and creators who naturally yoke multiple skill sets and varied perspectives in one personality? We ended the last chapter with an overarching set of characteristics describing a genuine school of creativity. Two of those traits come into play here:

○ They feature cross-curricular and multidisciplinary work more than subject-specific work.
○ They address the many multiple intelligences both separately and in creative blends.

And seen in the light of these two attributes, the third characteristic also becomes fundamental:

○ They feature a faculty who are themselves expert in their fields, creating multiple master-and-apprentice opportunities.

From the outside looking in, these three elements of schooling creativity may not seem so groundbreaking, but you only need to examine the standard American high school to grasp what a true paradigm shift this represents. High school is where everything from scheduling to credit hours are governed by lockstep subject-area requirements that are focused almost solely on the development of Linguistic and Logical-Mathematical Intelligences. And even those two intellectual domains are taught in silos with linguistic fluency addressed solely in English and occasionally in social studies courses, while logical-mathematical training is ruled by the math department, with an occasional assist from a science teacher.

The other seven of Gardner's nine intelligences are relegated to elective courses from physical education to band, including what are typically labeled "vocational" courses like drafting or nursing. It is truly no wonder that what most of us remember about the high school years is not school but the interpersonal and intrapersonal adventures that happened when we skipped class or somehow evaded our parents' watchful eyes. In terms of engagement with the learning process and dedicated focus on a task, the sociologist Herb Childress said it best in his famous article titled "Seventeen Reasons Why Football Is Better Than High School." After spending a year studying the sociology of high school, Childress noted that students almost universally reported boredom as their number one experience regardless of academic standing:

> What I saw mostly—and what the students told me about most frequently—was not learning at all but boredom. I saw students talking in class, not listening to lectures, having conversations instead of working on their study guides, putting their heads on their desks, and tuning out. Teachers talked about what a struggle it was to get students to turn in their homework at all, much less on time. Students picked up enough information to pass the test, did their work well enough to get the grade, and then totally forgot whatever it can be said that they had learned.

Childress discovered that the problem was not inside the students but inside the school. In fact, it was only in where they went and what they did after school that most students found meaning and focus.

In fact, what we serve up in the typical middle and high school experience is about as unimaginative and uninspiring as it could possibly be. Even when we cry up Innovation or Application, we do so through the same medium of subject-area specificity typically taught by the most authoritarian means possible. Furthermore, the final arbiter of academic success is always a number, whether it be a grade point average or a test score.

But enough. What is a creative, twenty-first-century answer to this outdated model?

Coached Project Classrooms

The primary path back to meaningful teaching and learning must involve devoting most of the school day to cross-curricular, multidisciplinary work that results in authentic products and performances created by students. As a result of our extended study of APA's learner-centered psychological principles in the 1990s, we developed a detailed description of the Paideia Coached Project that is intended to blend multiple subject areas into one body of ongoing student work. Furthermore, the school for creativity asks students to work in concert to produce a product for an authentic audience that is the result of multiple drafts or rehearsals—much as a musical chorus or athletic team prepares for and presents a concert or game performance. The driving force behind this idea is that students desperately need the opportunity to develop and showcase their best work in response to a challenge.

The important thing to note in this context is that the teacher takes on the role of a coach—whether it be writing coach, research partner, construction foreman, or drama director—while the students do the vast majority of the work. If there is one obvious metaphor for the teacher in a Coached Project classroom it is that of master to apprentice. She is involved in leading the work, but the students themselves bring their own imagination and passion to the production, and no two performances are alike. In short, class work is not standardized but personalized by each group of students.

The Human Body: A Middle School Project

Take as an example a middle school project that began in science and health classrooms but immediately overflowed into language arts and even mathematics. Along the way, this project, titled "The Human Body: Systems We Are Made Of," provided inspiration to at least five of Gardner's original nine intelligences. The project is designed to involve seventh-grade students in the active and relevant (!) production of two related products:

- The creation and execution of a personal fitness plan by each student based on the personal health data collected as part of the project.
- The collection and publication of a wide range of health-related data from all seventh-grade students organized by the primary systems in the human body—titled "The Profile of a Seventh Grader."

The project consists of two simultaneous strands: one individualized strand wherein each student develops a personal health plan and records his or her success in following it over a period of weeks, and a second wherein the entire class collects a wide range of health-related data to create a group portrait of the seventh-grade class at their school.

The group data collection and portrait is the work of six semi-autonomous work teams, each advised by a medical or physical education professional: muscular, skeletal, cardiovascular, nervous, digestive, and respiratory systems. The two primary audiences for this product are the local school board (who are in charge of establishing local physical education requirements) and the state Department of Public Instruction (who are in charge of setting state-level education policy).

The creative aspect of this work is that it is a fully integrated middle school project designed specifically for implementation by a middle school team or, at the very least, by the science, math, and physical education teachers at that grade level working in close collaboration with the students. Although this project is built around typical middle school science and math curricula, it also has obvious ramifications for the physical education and language arts departments. The idea is that students lose track of the hard and fast distinctions between the subject areas as they work to complete both individual and team work to the highest level of quality.

Note that in addition to the six groups or teams of students that take on the more specific task of studying various bodily systems, there is a seventh team whose job is to provide ongoing quality control information on the relative progress of the work. In other words, there is a group of students whose job consists of studying the various teams and their progress toward finished data collection on the overall health of the seventh-grade student body. In so doing, they operationalize group as well as individual assessment that is ongoing and collaborative—all with the end products in mind.

Finally, there is a core component to this project that provides the reflection that complements the action. There are three Paideia Seminar discussions built into the structure of the project: one on the human skeleton; a second on the comparison of the traditional Food Pyramid versus the more recent Willett and Skerrett "Healthy Eating Pyramid"; and a third on Leonardo da Vinci's *Vitruvian*

Man, along with the notes that accompanied the diagram in da Vinci's journal. Although the first two of these seminar texts are predominantly science and physical education focused, the third, the *Vitruvian Man*, cuts across all of the academic subjects engaged by this project: science, math, physical education, and language arts. In other words, it is inspired by and inspires a discussion of at least six of Gardner's original multiple intelligences: Linguistic, Logical-Mathematical, Spatial, Bodily-Kinesthetic, Interpersonal, and Intrapersonal.

By extension, the entire project addresses not only multiple intelligences, including the traditional Linguistic and Logical-Mathematical, but also treats these multiple ways of thinking and understanding as woven together rather than artificially isolated. Finally, there is an expert role to be played by most if not all the faculty on the middle school team, including the physical education teacher as well as the math, science, and language arts teachers. The idea of a "master" teaching her craft to a team of apprentices plays out naturally through the project work.

Citizenship: A High School Project

The original intent of middle school design (as opposed to the old-fashioned junior high school) was to encourage this sort of cross-curricular work. It obviously becomes more difficult in the standard high school setting where, if anything, academic subjects are even more balkanized than they were in the 1980s when Arthur G. Powell, David K. Cohen, and Eleanor Farrar skewered the American high school in *The Shopping Mall High School: Winners and Losers in the Educational Marketplace*. Recent trends in high school reform (such as the "new school" movement sponsored by the Bill and Melinda Gates Foundation) have left the traditional academic subjects largely separate and untouched.

Even in this more traditional environment, however, it's possible to create student work that is authentic, even inspiring. Consider this high school project that lives primarily in American history and civics classes but in the end outgrows the high school itself. It is designed to involve students from a number of classes in the production of three related products during an election year:

- Hosting a debate among local candidates in which they are questioned closely on their views concerning issues relevant to local voters.
- Publication and distribution of a Voters' Guide to local, state, and national elections.
- Publication and distribution of a "trifold" summary of local, state, and national candidates for voter use at the polls on election day.

The original candidates' debate, hosted by students, serves as one method of collecting information about the candidates, to be documented in detail in the Voters' Guide and summarized in the Candidate Summary.

The debate, as well as the resulting Voters' Guide and Candidate Summary, is designed to be the work of seven semiautonomous work teams (which give students a wide variety of intriguing roles): debate production/quality control, local school board elections, local city council and county commissioner elections, state representative elections, state executive elections, state and/or federal judicial elections, and federal congressional elections. (Obviously, this list can be adjusted to fit different scenarios in different years; a presidential election team can be added and other teams created or deleted as needed.) The debate production/quality control team is responsible for planning and directing the local debate and overseeing project quality control throughout.

This project is intended to be carried out by a typical set of high school civics or US history classes working in concert; however, it involves important ingredients from language arts, and the potential is here for a rich partnership between history and English teachers. Furthermore, students engaged in this work must practice many of the skills and habits of mind that lead directly to active and informed citizenship; therefore, the project will fit appropriately into almost any citizenship education program. Finally, this project is designed around the US Constitution. In one sense, its purpose is to teach the Constitution as the background to all contemporary elections, whether local, state, or federal—because it is the ideas and values of the Constitution that undergird our notions of a functional, representative democracy.

For that reason, the Constitution itself is the text for a series of Paideia Seminars, during which students dig into the actual words of the Constitution in order to construct their own detailed understanding of that seminal document. In this way, student reflection fuels student action, and student work is informed by profound thought and discussion.

It is also important to note that the audience for these products—debate, Voters' Guide, Candidate Summary—is quite real. It consists of those citizens in the community who will go to the polls on election day. The goal with all three of these products is to provide utterly objective and nonpartisan information, which voters can then use to inform their own trip to the voting booth. This approach is vital because it trains the students to investigate the candidates and what they stand for and to analyze the positions those candidates adopt, regardless of political party or faction. The students are learning citizenship by practicing it at the most fundamental level while simultaneously developing their critical thinking and literacy skills. As exciting as this type of authentic work is to both students and teachers, it is all too rare in academic courses across the world's secondary schools, including American high schools.

Additional Examples of Project-Based Instruction

As prevalent as it is, the paradigm of the conventional high school is not universal. There are already startling and successful exceptions to the rule. Since 2001, Federal Hocking High School in Stewart, Ohio, has shattered the traditional path through the high school grades by requiring all students not only to complete senior projects on subjects that interest them (which is reasonably common across the country) but also to serve parts of their junior and senior years in off-campus internships designed to encourage exploration and creativity. In addition, many students also complement their academic coursework by formally taking on various jobs on as well as off campus. Some might dismiss this approach as the naïve answer to twenty-first-century problems, only possible in a small school district in rural middle America.

But consider William Smith High School in Aurora, Colorado. William Smith is an Expeditionary Learning school that serves a large and diverse population of students under the motto "Students Choose the Life They Wish to Lead." The William Smith mission is based entirely on project-based work where "students are engaged in multi-grade level, cross-content projects, choosing to spend their day engaged in one project at a time, or working on several projects at once. In these projects, students work on and learn content as well as gain important academic and 21st Century skills, such as *collaboration, creativity, problem solving, and innovation*" (William Smith High School website, emphasis added). Even more impressive is that William Smith teachers plan these projects based in part on student feedback so that they strike a strong balance between academic standards and student interest. As with Federal Hocking

High School, part of what's significant is what's missing: a lack of emphasis on subject-area specialization and traditional academic success measured by AP classes and student GPA. And despite this authentic training for life in a fractured twenty-first-century world, William Smith boasts a 95 percent daily attendance rate as well as a 90 percent graduation rate and sends its students to prestigious colleges and universities.

The same trend holds true at the Chattanooga School for the Arts and Sciences, along with its partner school the Chattanooga School for the Liberal Arts, in Chattanooga, Tennessee, where rigorous academics are the norm without reference to traditional metrics. At CSAS and CSLA, middle and high school courses are increasingly taught with a consistent emphasis on project-based instruction, and student production or performance is balanced by the consistent use of Paideia Seminar discussion, so that students are constantly engaged in the alternating practice of action and reflection while learning.

All these schools represent a forward-looking movement in public education, where students are taught to recognize and blend their multiple intelligences in creative and productive ways. In a sense, education in these schools is not an end unto itself (higher test scores, more intense specialization) but rather a means to an end—and that end is a productive life.

CHAPTER 12

COACHING INDIVIDUALITY AND TEAMWORK

Most creative individuals like to work alone *and* as a member of a team. At first glance, that statement seems contradictory, but consider this: The creative personality enjoys the opportunity to strike out on her own—paint in new colors, strike new poses, exclaim in new voices—but often she procures the emotional support for this sort of risk-taking from others who recognize her for who she is and support her venture into the unknown. In addition, the creative personality often draws inspiration from the work of others.

Perhaps the best example of this once again comes from the world of jazz. Typically, there is a horn section and a rhythm section in a jazz combo. The horn section might consist of saxophones, trumpets, and trombones, and the rhythm section might consist of piano, bass, guitar, and drums. But all of this is flexible, and then there is the clarinet who wandered in at the last moment. The jazz ensemble might be large (an entire band) or small (a few friends jamming on their instruments). And when they get warmed up, the essence of the music emerges, and that essence is improvisation. Jazz musicians leave the traditional score far behind, each playing his riff both with and without the others. They take inspiration from one another and then soar into individual space. In short, they are both alone and together. The one feeds the other.

Schools don't typically work this way. The number one reason they don't is the vast and invasive evaluation system that pits teacher against teacher and student against student—always emphasizing the individual achievement and ignoring or even punishing the collective effort. There is a saying in the education profession that what matters is what gets tested. Unfortunately, the converse is also true: what gets tested ends up being what matters. Sadly, the vast majority of academic tests pit one student against all others or, at the very least, measure one student's growth against that of all others. For this reason, we are constantly measuring and comparing, and the end result is that most schools in America have become the equivalent of giant sorting machines, which eventually churn out high school graduates with a variety of bewildering numbers stamped all over them. If you can't see those numbers with the naked eye, trust me, they are there. Simply request a transcript.

WHY TEAMWORK IS ESSENTIAL IN CREATIVE SCHOOLS

The current dedication to both standardization and individual competition flies in the face of everything we know about creativity and the development of the creative personality. Remember the jazz combo. Or the dance troupe. Or the theater group. Or, for that matter, the state championship soccer team. All of which feature spontaneity and teamwork, resulting in the proper meshing of the individual and the group. We need schools that recognize and reward novelty and spontaneity, both from the individual and the ensemble.

Revisiting our earlier description of Creative Schools, we find that:

○ They offer ample opportunity for students to work in teams as well as through individual performance.

○ They stress group and individual assessment that is ongoing and collaborative rather than standardized and summative.

Both of which characteristics lead us to:

○ They stress quality production and performance based on multiple drafts or repeated practices and rehearsals.

It goes almost without saying that most incidences of multiple drafts, repeated practices, or rehearsals involve the group as well as the individual. And furthermore, the group performance ultimately matters as much as the individual product.

This notion that we must stress the social nature of creative schooling takes us back to the American Psychological Association's findings about how our species learns. First, there is the individual (principle 7):

Curiosity, creativity, and higher-order thinking are stimulated by relevant, authentic learning tasks of optimal difficulty and novelty for each student.

And then there is the individual working with others (principle 10):

Learning and self-esteem are heightened when individuals are in respectful and caring relationships with others who see their potential, genuinely appreciate their unique talents, and accept them as individuals.

In such an environment, the group is inspired by the individual insight, and the individual galvanized by the group vision.

COLLABORATIVE DIVERGENT THINKING

Nowhere is this fundamental law of learning more obvious than in Paideia Seminar discussion as it is currently practiced. By definition, the Paideia Seminar is a collaborative, intellectual dialogue facilitated through open-ended questions about a text. Note the prominence of the word *collaborative*, as opposed to competitive. *Intellectual* here means that the discussion is about concepts rather than facts. The facilitator uses primarily *open-ended questions* to involve as many participants in the collective thinking and talking as possible and to inspire a range of responses. In other words, divergent thinking is the norm in a seminar. Finally, a *text* in this case may be any human artifact that embodies a rich web of ideas.

Imagine, for example, a primary grades science seminar on Aesop's fable "The Crow and the Pitcher." Or an elementary math seminar on "Pascal's Triangle," an early computing tool in graphic form associated with Blaise Pascal. Or a middle grades social studies seminar on an illustrated page from *The Egyptian Book of the Dead*. Or a high school English seminar on a lyric by Sappho. The list goes on and on, but what all of these texts have in common is their incredible richness of ideas and their fundamental ambiguity. Both of these characteristics—intellectual complexity and ambiguity—open up the text to multiple interpretations, which in turn means that students are invited to create new and different explanations of what the text means and how.

When you combine textual ambiguity with truly open-ended questions from a skilled facilitator, the result is the widest possible range of perspectives, which students can then synergize in increasingly sophisticated ways. The open-ended nature of seminar questions is especially significant in this context, because in the traditional classroom of the last 50 years "teacher questions" have been almost exclusively designed to lead students to the one right answer, the predetermined curricular point. In other words, teachers have constructed questions—consciously or unconsciously—to drive convergent thinking and discourage divergent thinking. This practice has become all the more common in the age of high-stakes testing, where only one answer to a multiple-choice test question is the right one.

The Paideia Seminar, on the other hand, rejects this long-standing trend by featuring both texts and questioning strategies intended to inspire a wide range of student answers, which can then be blended into much more complex points of view. In the world of the seminar circle, intellectual creativity is not just accepted—it is the norm. For that reason, assessment in a Paideia classroom features the sort of student writing that allows for the full range of creative expression.

Why Seminars Offer a Richer Learning Experience

The seminar experience drives individual creativity through the complexity of the group response—and vice versa. The result of a wide-ranging and fluent seminar discussion is a synthesis of multiple perspectives that is more sophisticated and explains more of the world than any one person's insight did in the beginning. This phenomenon explains why, when we ask a group of seminar participants how many of them understand the text better after the seminar than before, most or all raise their hands and can then go on to explain that growing understanding.

This intellectual symbiosis feeds the creative individual like few other classroom activities. For that reason, students display marked improvement in many areas after a seminar: writing is more sophisticated and coherent, artwork is more complex and varied, problem solving is more fluid and creative, and self-awareness and mindfulness in relation to others is more nuanced and mature.

As an experienced high school seminar participant once remarked to me in an interview, "Over time, you learn to think like a seminar," which I interpret to mean that as an individual you learn first to think synthetically by blending multiple, even contradictory, ideas. And as you grow further accustomed to this sort of creative thinking, you begin to think symphonically, such that the multitude of ideas expressed through different voices or instruments is blended into something rich and novel—perhaps even something beautiful.

CHANGING HOW WE EVALUATE PROGRESS

The case was presented earlier that what gets tested is invariably what matters. In order to encourage the sort of creative thinking demanded by our world, we must change the way we evaluate student work and student progress. We must learn to assess the production of the team as well as the work of the individuals on the team. In the context of the Paideia Seminar, teachers commonly create group process goals against which the group, through discussion and writing, can appraise its own progress. This serious work then allows students to self-assess, with the teacher's help, how they as individuals are contributing to the evolving maturity of the group. Seminar facilitators also ask students to consciously incorporate the ideas and language of fellow students into their own speaking, writing, and problem solving, and along the way give credit where credit is due. In other words, Paideia teachers find multiple ways to use measurement to encourage both collaboration as well as individual creativity—neither of which is currently valued by how we track student growth.

This brings us to a third characteristic of the Creative School that is related to the simultaneous development of the individual and the group: these schools "stress quality production and performance based on multiple drafts and repeated practices and rehearsals." For the past decade or so, the term *rigor* has been on fire in educational circles, meaning that school officials are constantly calling for more academic rigor; we must have high expectations for all students and reject shoddy or lazy work. Fair enough, but this is easy to demand and hard to achieve. What "rigor" actually means in practical terms is slowing down enough to coach students as they write multiple drafts of an essay, perform multiple iterations of a lab experiment, research not just primary but also secondary sources for history projects, and practice group performances with the same painstaking attention to detail as the football team (remember the article "Seventeen Reasons Why Football Is Better Than High School"). Creative teaching is often slow teaching, and creative learning is often slow learning.

In order to get to a new focus on multiple drafts and rehearsals, we have to stop making tests the climax of the school day or week or year and start focusing on how slow, formative assessment—collaborative and ongoing—is the key to slow, incremental improvement. Further—and this is where the current education establishment will struggle the most—we have to stop standardizing both the measurement tools and the targeted results. As long as we ask the same things of all students, we will get the same things from all students. Abject boredom will be the result because passion and creativity will find someplace away from school to flourish.

The reason this emphasis on slow and collaborative assessment is so important is because it is precisely how good writing becomes truly creative writing, how a gift for bodily-kinesthetic expression becomes brilliant dance or athletic performance, how a group of musicians becomes an orchestra, how an architect and a builder who only just met collaborate to produce an illuminating space, and how a photographer and her model collaborate through the lens of a camera. There are a hundred examples, but the point is that creativity is born in rehearsal and given expression in perfor

And without the rehearsal, the draft, the practice, the getting it wrong over and over before getting it right, the final product is barren.

———

Creators make things. They are bored by tests and have little interest in the results. Rather, the end result of their play or work is a product or performance of value to themselves and others. Ultimately, the quality, the novelty of that performance is the true measure of their commitment and their inspiration. Our challenge is to reimagine and redesign schools so that we redistribute the thousands of hours we have devoted to tests and the equally chilling preparation for tests.

Instead, we must learn how to give equal time and attention to the rigor of the process as well as the product. Equal time to the individual and her role as it evolves within the group. And in every case, we must celebrate the new and novel response as superior to the tried and true.

CHAPTER 13

FEEDING THE CREATIVE PERSONALITY

Ambitious . . . focused . . . asynchronous . . . marginal . . . resilient . . . pro-
ductive. These are the adjectives that we discovered early on in our
exploration of the creative personality. The final question we have
to answer about a school that nurtures creativity is how it might feed
these personality traits rather than starve them.

In an earlier era of tumult and unrest, Ralph Waldo Emerson
gave us a startlingly fresh description of the graduate of such a
school:

> A sturdy lad from New Hampshire or Vermont, who in
> turn tries all the professions, who teams it, farms it, ped-
> dles, keeps a school, preaches, edits a newspaper, goes to
> Congress, buys a township, and so forth, in successive years,
> and always like a cat falls on his feet, is worth a hundred of
> these city dolls. He walks abreast with his days and feels no
> shame in not "studying a profession," for he does not post-
> pone his life, but lives already. He has not one chance, but
> a hundred chances.

So apt is this description from his essay "Self-Reliance"—written more than 175 years ago—that it serves almost as a case study of the sturdy individuals who will flourish in 2050. They grow under pressure rather than shrink. They unfold new facets of skill and interest rather than clinging to outdated modes. They continue to amplify and mature long into the marathon that is life. In short, theirs is an ongoing and lifelong evolution, with the occasional revolution thrown in for good measure.

As a result, they have not one but a hundred chances.

THE ATTRIBUTES OF CREATIVE SCHOOLS

There are four attributes of a school that nurture this personality in particular:

- They stress quality production and performance based on multiple drafts or repeated practices and rehearsals.
- They teach the use of technology for research or production and discourage internet and social media distractions.
- They feature learning experiences that foster resilience and focus rather than compliance and certainty.
- They create these experiences for all students, not for a select few.

Quality Production and Performance

The first of these four characteristics—quality product or performance—seems almost a given, and yet it is incredibly rare in the world of the contemporary American middle or high school. There are papers to be turned in, quizzes and tests to take, and labs to be completed, but rarely is there true project work leading to a product of real-world value, except in what used to be called vocational classes. Students did real work in everything from nursing to auto mechanics to masonry to drafting, with perhaps the supreme examples being those carpentry classes that built houses as part of a live project or those food service classes that operated a catering business out of the school kitchen. These examples are rare enough, and very little of that sort of authentic production is associated with academic classes, especially when you add the caveat that the work should be produced for an audience outside the classroom and that the emphasis should be on a collective rather than an individual product.

Of all those requirements, the live audience is quite probably the most rigorous arbiter of authenticity, because almost all academic work is produced for and graded by the teacher, so that it is locked into an endless cycle of irrelevance that contributes to the students' overwhelming sense of boredom. By high school, certainly, most students correctly feel that the work they do in core academic classes is largely divorced from the world outside school, and the result is the general malaise described by Herb Childress in "Seventeen Reasons Why Football Is Better Than High School." Some students will continue to perform, jumping through teacher-held hoops in hopes of scoring a high GPA or class rank, with the ultimate nirvana of choice college admissions. But even those students will tell you, if asked candidly, that the work itself is largely meaningless outside that context.

One way of combating that malaise is to make algebra more like masonry, biology more like nursing, American history more like live-project research, and learning to write in English class a matter of publication. What follows is a simple list of possible products and performances that various middle and high school teachers have used over the years to inject a strong dose of reality into academic coursework. It is far from comprehensive, but it does serve to suggest the possibilities.

POSSIBLE ACADEMIC PRODUCTS and PERFORMANCES

Written Products and Performances	Auditory Products and Performances	Visual Products and Performances	Other Products and Performances
Advertisement	Audiotape	Blueprint	Art Exhibit
Biography	Choral Reading	Cartoon	Dance Choreography
Blog	Debate	Collage	Election Guide
Book Review	Dramatization	Computer Graphic	Historical Structure Renovation
Brochure	Interview	Computer-Generated Presentation	Mural
Directions	Musical Composition	Data Table	Outdoor Expedition
Editorial	Newscast	Design	Quilt
Essay	Oral Presentation	Diagram	Set Design
Experiment	Panel Discussion	Display	Stream Watch Program
Game	Play	Diorama	Sundial
Journal	Podcast	Drawing	Water Testing Kit
Lab Report	Poetry Reading	Graphic Novel	Website
Letter	Rap	Map	Wildlife Brochures & Checklists
Logbook	Readers' Theater	Mime	
Magazine Article	Skit	Model	
Newspaper Article	Song	Painting	
Novel	Storytelling Festival	Photo Essay	
Poem	Teaching a Lesson	Scrapbook	
Proposal		Sculpture	
Questionnaire		Slideshow	
Research Report		Storyboard	
Screenplay		Videotape	
Script			
Short Story			
Textbook			

All of these student productions have in common the potential for an authentic audience beyond the walls of the classroom and, in many instances, the walls of the school. This is vital because it provides an equally authentic element of quality control based not on the grade assigned by the teacher but on the response of that audience to the product. The teacher is free to assume the role of master craftsman (editor, researcher, scientist, mathematician, musician, coach) in relation to the students as apprentices, and both teacher and students are invested in the quality of the final product.

The point of this radical shift in perspective is that it removes student work from the boring and artificial world of papers, tests, and quizzes—all of which are intended to rank order them as individuals—and gives that work the authority and legitimacy of real-world performance.

This sort of performance-based teaching and learning has long been the purview of both training in the arts and training in the vocations—especially hands-on vocations. It is also the pedagogical creed of athletic coaches and trainers. In all of these areas of human learning, it is assumed by all concerned that practice is what leads to rigor, not native ability. And further, practice almost always assumes that the students, the workers, the athletes must fail before they can succeed. At the very least, they must suffer through the multiple drafts, the seemingly endless rehearsals, the brutal training sessions before mastering either the art or the craft.

This devotion to practice before perfection means slowing down the current educational milieu, which is devoted to speed and coverage. It also means that the goal of any classroom—indeed, any school—is to produce teams of students who are greater than the sum of their parts. These students will know how to work both together and alone—at times merging their best work into that of the ensemble and at times singing solo.

Use of Technology for Research—But Not
Allowing It to Become a Distraction

This kind of project-based schooling has clear implications for the use of technology as a tool for production, not as a replacement for the teacher or as a social distraction. In short, a school that is designed to nurture the creative personality must make technology training part of its curriculum, but not so much for the sake of teaching "coding" or training IT engineers but as a way of building creative competence with technology as a tool—for filmmaking, for publishing, for graphic design, for musical composition, and so on.

One of the things we know about the creative temperament is that at its best it is both ambitious and focused—with an emphasis here on *focused*. In recent years, it has become increasingly obvious that the personal, handheld device—yes, I mean your iPhone—is both a curse and a blessing in that it provides both a steady diet of dopamine thrill from social media plus the potential for instantaneous communication with a wide variety of people. In other words, it can be and often is a world-class distraction. It's not how creative work gets done; it's how creative work gets postponed. For that reason alone, it is necessary that we teach the next generation of students how to use their personal devices rather than *being used by them*—with the ultimate goal of constructing new and different means of portraying and understanding the world.

The individual who designs a new app is the creator; the thousands of people who use it are merely consumers. The individual who will thrive in 2050 is the creator.

Seen in this light, technology might be a means to the productive end of almost any student project, just as a slide rule, a typewriter, or a darkroom once was. Or a library. One danger presented to any creative individual by the internet is the availability of ready-made information on almost any topic. Without delving too deeply into the relative worth or validity of most of the information available on the internet, its greatest danger may be that it is already chewed and digested, synthesized and packaged. In other words, the thinking has been done, or at least it would appear so, and the result is the intellectual equivalent of baby food. This deceptive facet of internet research is part of being used by technology rather than making use of it, and part of teaching technology as a tool is teaching its limitations. By definition, the next-generation creator thinks for herself rather than having that thinking done and delivered to her via a device.

Resilience and Focus

Students need to engage with primary texts of all kinds through seminar discussion, and they must then use the insights they themselves produce to construct and perform new work. This is where seminar dialogue—as shared reflection—feeds the rigorous demands of authentic production. In this way, it is possible to teach resilience through multiple discussions, ongoing self-assessment, and multiple drafts or rehearsals. Our collective work is never as good as it's going to be if we allow the time and space for slow, incremental improvement. And in many significant instances, the best teaching and learning is slow teaching and learning.

Creative Experiences for ALL Students

The last element of the school for creativity involves not what but *who*; it creates the experiences we've described here *for all students, not for a select few*. One of the most unfortunate results of our decades-long love affair with "intelligence" as a measurable quotient is that we fell prey to the notion that we should identify the "gifted" among us at an early age and single them out for the most interesting programming, the best teachers, and the most inspiring experiences. We believed we should value them by accelerating them.

If there is one thing that Howard Gardner's work on both multiple intelligences and creativity reveals it's that we can't predict just who will develop into the creative genius. First of all, we don't know how to test for those traits with any validity; second, creativity is often a late-blooming quality built out of life experience. By its very nature, it is unpredictable.

The implications for this bald truth are as follows: One, creative teaching and learning need to move to the core of all schools, not just those devoted to the arts or schools of choice that tout their focus on innovation. Two, creativity is the subject of all disciplinary study, not to be relegated to the status of an elective middle or high school course. Rather, it permeates the way we learn just about everything, including math and science. Three, and most important of all, it is the educative birthright of every child who walks in the schoolhouse door. We must nurture ambition and focus, comfort with asynchrony and marginality, resilience in the face of early failure, and a dedication to authentic productivity—in all children and adolescents. The days of tracked classes and weighted courses are over. They are not just narrow and unlovely; they are self-defeating in every way.

———

The schools that recognize the challenges of the future have these qualities:

- They feature cross-curricular and multidisciplinary work more than subject-specific work.
- They address the many multiple intelligences both separately and in creative blends.
- They feature a faculty who are themselves expert in their fields, creating multiple master-and-apprentice opportunities.

○ They offer ample opportunity for students to work in teams as well as through individual performance.

○ They stress group and individual assessment that is ongoing and collaborative rather than standardized and summative.

○ They stress quality production and performance based on multiple drafts or repeated practices and rehearsals.

○ They teach the use of technology for research or production and discourage internet and social media distractions.

○ They feature learning experiences that foster resilience and focus rather than compliance and certainty.

○ They create these experiences for all students, not for a select few.

What we now see is that this vision of education for creativity is not a pipe dream or a fairy tale. In many places, these schools have sprung into being—in reaction against the status quo and in anticipation of the life for which they are preparing their students.

It only remains for us to turn away from the past and devote our energies to the future.

Part Three

WHAT NOW? WHAT NEXT?

CHAPTER 14

CREATIVITY AS A
UNIQUE PATH

This exploration of twenty-first-century capacity began by asking what might replace the word and, along with the word, the idea of *smart*. If the notion of intelligence as a static and measurable attribute has begun to limit us, what would we replace it with?

Out of that question emerged the idea of *creative* as the most compelling replacement for *smart*. But not just creative as yet one more inherent attribute for which one individual scores higher on a scale than another. Rather, creativity as a set of traits that can be developed by most people and expressed in a wide variety of ways.

This new paradigm for human achievement is so immediate and authentic because it is precisely what the constantly shifting world around us demands. The question of who will thrive in 2050 is pertinent to *now* as well as *then*, for the seeds of the asynchronous world described in chapter 4 are scattered abroad in our own lives and taking root all around us.

Perhaps, then, the most disturbing thing about what has been said thus far is that the creative individual who will flourish in this world is precisely that—an individual. She will not be defined by a metric or a type; she will not be measured by a grade point average or an annual income. In fact, the most creative among us will find ways to blow up the traditional measures of success even as they touch them.

What does it mean to recognize and value the individual among us? Even more to the point, what does it mean to find and nurture the individual lurking within each of us?

Recall that a core element in Howard Gardner's profile of exemplary creators involved the necessity of marginality in creative lives. Some creators are marginalized by birth, some by income or social class, some by shifting political or cultural values, some by gender or race, but regardless of the reason, the sense of being on the outside looking in predominates. Furthermore, Gardner discovered that creators needed their marginality because it fed their work: "Whenever they risked becoming members of 'the establishment,' they would again shift course to attain at least intellectual marginality" (368).

In other words, creators fight to maintain their independent perspective, even rejecting the siren songs of success—money and status—in the constant battle to remain fresh and novel. They leave home for unknown countries or cultures. They retreat from the public eye into private haunts. They embark on new relationships and form new families. They embrace new challenges. Like Tennyson's Ulysses, they abandon even the throne in order "to strive, to seek, to find."

This devotion to individuality and the independent search for expression is so important now because it is the only way forward available to us. There is no longer a ready-made road to success of any kind; one must cut the path rather than taking a well-traveled route. That in turn means that to be successful, each one of us must respond again and again to the world with spontaneity, reimagining and recreating ourselves as necessary.

The ability to do this requires a certain amount of shape-shifting over the course of a lifetime, but it is shape-shifting carried out while still being true to one's core psychological attributes. Or to say it another way, the successful individual will express his own unique personality traits by continuously growing and recombining them.

What does this mean in real terms? That each of us—in this generation as well as the next—must learn to practice divergent thinking as a form of self-discipline. Rather than converging on the answers provided by the example of others, we must each learn to ask new questions and to do so with what Oliver Sacks calls "special audacity [and] subversiveness." The second important thing that our brave new world demands of us is that we each learn how to diversify and blend our talents. The age of specialization is dying as you read this.

Recall Gardner's list of his seven prototypical creators and how each embodied an especially productive fusion of intelligences: Martha Graham with her astonishing mix of bodily and linguistic abilities, Mahatma Gandhi with his charismatic personal and linguistic skills, Albert Einstein with his logical-spatial vision combined with musical and even existential ingenuity. When we begin to examine the truly creative among us, we almost invariably discover that they yoke together specialties or disciplines in unexpected and even unique ways.

Furthermore, they manage these multiple ways of understanding the world without becoming either fragmented or rigid. Indeed, if anything, they become more fully integrated through their individuality. And because they fuse multiple ways of responding to new challenges, they are more flexible and more resilient than those individuals who have only one way of seeing and understanding what the world presents them with.

This combination of divergent thinking with multifaceted intelligence is the reason why success in our fractured world is more a matter of profile than profession. Professions will come and go in the next 30, 40, 50 years. They are neither static nor dependable.

What will not change is change itself, except that it will become more rapid and more variable.

For this reason, the young women and men who will graduate from high school and college in coming years must learn to live from the inside out rather than the outside in. The more fragmented and disorienting the outside world, the greater the need for an inner coherence and self-assurance. Rather than accepting the world's definition of career and success—living from the outside in—they each must look within for what is a unique blend of intellect and talent and learn how to express that individual power in as wide a variety of ways as possible.

Individuality is an expression of both insight and will, and that expression—stubborn yet pliable—will be the key to success in the coming decades.

We need to prepare ourselves for the spectacular challenges of a long life that is volatile and fractured but, as a result, rich with possibility. The prodigy is often exhausted by midlife and the fire of the lyric poet burned down to cinders. The sensibility of the sage, on the other hand, grows only deeper and more sophisticated through decades of productivity—and thus is well-suited to starting over. And over.

We need to educate our children—both in school and out—for the tests provided by life over many decades. This preparation means that we will help them develop a creative profile rather than train for a profession: the profile of a blended, ambitious, resilient generalist who is capable of good work in a variety of complex environments. For parents, this means not protecting children and adolescents from struggle as well as helping them learn to take risks over their long and productive lives. Although we may not live to see it, they will become the sages of their day and age.

This, then, is the portrait of a sage in the making—those creative individuals who are constantly emerging and producing:

○ *They will blend multiple intelligences in a way that might be described as synthetic or even symphonic.*

○ *They will be ambitious and focused without being self-obsessed.*

○ *They will value asynchrony and even seek it out.*

○ *They will use their own marginality to generate a novel perspective and new work.*

○ *They will exhibit a steadfast resilience in all phases of life.*

○ *They will be measured by what they produce over the course of their lives, not by any static notion of capacity or quotient.*

Perhaps another way of saying all this is that in the fractured world of 2050, only those among us who are creative will thrive because only the creative regard this constantly new and tumultuous life as an adventure.

NOTES

Introduction

Page 1

Lincoln on Liberty. Lincoln made these remarks in his address at a Sanitary Fair, Baltimore, April 18, 1864. The entire speech can be found in the *Collected Works of Abraham Lincoln*, volume 7 (pp. 301–3). It is worth noting that at this point, the nation had been embroiled in the Civil War for three years, and the issue of reaching some sort of agreement on the meaning of the most basic terms—like *liberty*—was paramount if the states were ever to be reunited.

Pages 3–4

Profile of the Creative Individual. This profile is inspired in part by Howard Gardner's profound 1993 "anatomy of creativity" titled *Creating Minds*. See specifically "A Portrait of the Exemplary Creator" (pp. 360–90). Although Gardner is best known for his work on multiple intelligences, this book-length study of seven archetypal creators from the early twentieth century is an extraordinarily important synthesis of powerful creative minds at work and speaks directly to the thesis of this book.

Chapter 1

Pages 7–8

Multiple Intelligences. Gardner's publication of *Frames of Mind* in 1983 caused a genuine paradigm shift in our understanding of human intelligence. He followed this initial salvo with two other important works: *The Mind's New Science* in 1987 and *The Unschooled Mind* in 1991. *The Unschooled Mind*, in particular, addressed how K through 12 education should ideally change in response to what Gardner and others were discovering about the multifaceted nature of intelligence. These works influenced what might be termed the multiple-intelligence movement in education in general (see Thomas Armstrong's *Multiple Intelligences in the Classroom*, for example) and the work of Harvard's Project Zero (http://www.pz.harvard.edu/) in particular.

Chapter 2

Pages 15–16

Creativity and Blended Intelligences. Although Gardner (in *Creating Minds*) recognizes that his archetypal creators exhibit a surprising "breadth and . . . combination of intelligences," he doesn't then go on to explore the relationship between creativity and blended intelligences in depth. That idea, however, has emerged in other, more recent biographical studies— like Walter Isaacson's *Leonardo da Vinci*—and illuminates the lives of other creative individuals from all areas of human endeavor.

Pages 19–20

Lifelong Learning and the Evolution of the Individual. The work of Robert Maynard Hutchins in introducing *The Great Books of the Western World* is fading from cultural consciousness as the whole notion of canonical "great books" has justifiably suffered repeated attacks for its lack of diversity. Even so, it's important to recall that Hutchins, along with Mortimer Adler and others, argued convincingly that the purpose of formal schooling was to prepare students to become educated over the course of their entire lifetimes. The classics were intended to be read and digested over many decades, and learning was best seen as "interminable." This resonates strongly with what Gardner and others have discovered by analyzing the lives of creative individuals, who typically continue to produce significant work into advanced old age.

Chapter 3

Pages 21–22

Love and Work. Sigmund Freud is widely attributed as the source for both these quotes about the primacy of love and work, including attributions from well-known psychologists like Erik Erikson and Mihaly Csikszentmihalyi. Ironically, however, they do not appear in Freud's writing nor in the written record of his conversation. Even so, they have become central to our ongoing dialogue about human health and happiness, so much so that the phrase has entered popular culture, often with Freud's name attached. Two modern novels, one by Reynolds Price (1968) and a second by Gwyneth Cravens (1982), have been titled *Love and Work*, though neither credits Freud.

Pages 22–23

Synthetic and Symphonic Intelligence. The use of the term *synthetic* to describe a type of intelligence stems from the common definition of *synthesis* as the combination of ideas or insights to form a more sophisticated explanation or theory. By extension, *synthetic thinking* is characterized by the effort to combine varied elements, even apparently contradictory elements, into a whole understanding greater than the sum of its parts. I use the term *symphonic* as an even more profound fusion of previously disparate parts into a unique whole. *Symphonic thinking*, then, weaves together many elements—threads, voices, instruments, movements, insights—into something rich and new.

Pages 24–25

Creativity and Communal Life. Doris Kearns Goodwin's portrait of Franklin and Eleanor Roosevelt (in *No Ordinary Time*) serves as a reminder to read and reread the (auto)biographies of those creators who were themselves capable of vibrant, even passionate, interpersonal lives and who defy the misanthropic stereotype. These include books like the following: Doris Kearns Goodwin's own portrait of Lincoln in *Team of Rivals* (2005); *The Lives of the Artists* by Giorgio Vasari (1551); *The Autobiography of Benjamin Franklin* (1791); *The Story of My Life* by Helen Keller (1903); Lynn Haney's *Naked at the Feast: A Biography of Josephine Baker* (1981); *Long Walk to Freedom* by Nelson Mandela (1994); *The Diary of Frida Kahlo: An Intimate Self-Portrait* (1995); Ron Chernow's *Alexander Hamilton* (2004), godfather to the contemporary musical; and many, many more.

Pages 25–27

Marginality. The term *marginality* or *marginalized* has become highly charged politically and culturally during the last decade—so much so that it is now almost impossible to imagine a white, male European or American who could claim to be in any way marginalized as the term is currently used. In this way, it is of course related to the phrases "white privilege" and "male privilege." I use it here following Gardner's earlier usage in his *Creating Minds*, published over 25 years ago. In this context, the term might refer to any individual who in the course of his or her life is thrust involuntarily from the cultural or social mainstream. Or, more significantly, any individual who chooses to step out of the mainstream voluntarily in order to gain perspective and creative independence. It is important to note that the ability to make that choice implies a certain amount of privilege—economic or otherwise—and always involves some risk. The point here is that many creative people are willing to take that risk in order to attempt new and compelling work.

Chapter 4

Page 32

Asynchrony. The word *synchronicity* has existed in popular culture since the June 1983 release of the album of the same name by the British rock band the Police. In essence, the word has to do with two or more things that happen simultaneously for a reason, usually not an obvious one. It dates back to the work of psychologist C. G. Jung, who was fascinated by the idea of hidden connections that generated psychic events (premonitions, shared mental images, and so on) that couldn't be explained by the traditional notions of cause and effect. It's not entirely clear what Jung believed about this phenomenon, except that he thought that human experience was much more consistent and connected than is commonly believed. All of this is to say that the experience of "asynchrony"—which will become increasingly common over the next 50 years—is, by definition, inconsistent and disconnected, unpredictable and so less controllable. Gardner uses the term in *Creating Minds* to introduce the idea that creative individuals seek out asynchrony because it is a social and cultural space rich with potential. The old order must pass away before a new one can be created.

Page 33

Decadence. The common definition of *decadence* is a state of being that is lazy, self-indulgent, lax—often as a result of a decline in duty or virtue. Jacques Barzun uses the term in a much more specific way—both in *The Culture We Deserve* (1989) and in his magnum opus, *From Dawn to Decadence: 1500 to the Present: 500 Years of Western Cultural Life* (2000)—to refer to periods in history when unifying forces dissolve and whole civilizations can perish as a result. Eventually, in Barzun's view (and that of many cultural historians), the death of one civilization eventually leads to the birth of others as new ideas of social order assert themselves. See, for example, Will and Ariel Durant's *The Lessons of History* (1968).

Pages 34–35

The Life Cycle of a Civilization. For a recent exploration of how a civilization that was once thought immortal passed out of existence, see Edward J. Watts's *Mortal Republic: How Rome Fell into Tyranny* (2018). Watts's study of the decline of Rome screams relevance to present-day authoritarian movements across the globe and reinforces the larger points made by cultural historians like Barzun and the Durants.

Page 36

Globalization. In part due to the impact of Thomas L. Friedman's *The World Is Flat*, "globalization" is often mistakenly viewed solely through the lens of economics. Although economic forces are obviously involved in the erosion of national borders and nationalist identities, there are many other factors, including religious, ethnic, and social forces that cut across national borders. In an era when almost universal social media and electronic communication is commonplace, these forces are increasingly powerful and must eventually reshape the metaphorical landscape, even for nations that have remained largely static entities for hundreds of years.

Chapter 5

Page 44

Sage. The use of the word *sage* (along with *sagacity* and *sagacious*) has declined in recent decades, so much so that the first definition that appears in most dictionaries refers to the plant rather than a person. Perhaps this is the result of the sage's association with experience and the wisdom gained thereby—which is often overlooked in the age of instantaneous access and information. I use it deliberately here to challenge the notion of creativity as the special province of the young. Ironically, in most areas other than lyric poetry, creativity appears to peak in waves throughout the many decades of life, making the wisdom gained by experience an especially valuable commodity in a long and challenging life. Seen in this light, the work of the sage will almost always be more sophisticated than that of the prodigy.

Page 48

Changing Family Life. It is no accident that one of the most popular sitcoms on current American television is titled simply *Modern Family*. The first episode aired in September 2009, and at the time of this writing, the show is in its tenth season. The extraordinary and long-running popularity of this comedy underlines just how much the traditional, biological family has evolved and continues to shift shape and membership. It also underscores how important flexibility and resilience are in creating healthy, loving relationships inside the sprawling and often messy world of the twenty-first-century family.

Chapter 6

Pages 56–57

Creators as Self-Taught. For creators who forge entirely new modes of expression, like the Greek historian Herodotus and the French essayist Michel de Montaigne, or fields of endeavor, like Sigmund Freud, autodidacticism is a necessity. Although most creators subvert traditional modes in an existing field, and therefore must study or even mimic conventional expression before departing from it, even they must teach themselves new forms in order to capture the fruit of their imaginations. Montaigne, on the other hand, had to manufacture an entirely new means of human expression to accommodate the scathingly honest and courageously deep exploration of his own personality. Like Freud, he doesn't get the credit he deserves as an archetypal creator. Sarah Bakewell's *How to Live: Or A Life of Montaigne in One Question and Twenty Attempts at an Answer* (2010) should be read in conjunction with the original essays (published in 1580 and countless editions since) as a case study of a tireless creator working in isolation to forge a new art form.

Chapter 7

Page 62

Youth versus Old Age. The World Health Organization (WHO) recently declared that 65 years of age is still considered young. Based on contemporary research on average health quality and life expectancy, it has defined the following categories of human aging:

0-17 years old: underage
18-65 years old: youth/young people
66-79 years old: middle-aged
80-99 years old: elderly/senior
100+ years old: long-lived elderly

Furthermore, the WHO claims that changes in social roles across developed countries is the primary factor in its reclassification. In other words, the WHO is officially recognizing that not only are people living longer, they are more active professionally and personally much later in life.

Page 64

Cognitive Disequilibrium. The idea of cognitive disequilibrium springs from Jean Piaget's work on child development. Piaget believed that as children develop they construct increasingly sophisticated schema, or mental representations of the world, which they then use both to understand and respond to situations. A state of equilibrium exists when a child's—or an adult's—schema functions successfully as a working explanation of what she encounters. In a fractured world like ours, psychic and cognitive disequilibrium is likely to become much more common as traditional roles and conventional assumptions lose their power to explain the world around us. One implication of this challenge is that adults will have to maintain their childlike ability to develop new and more powerful schema as their environments continue to shift and grow in complexity.

Chapter 8

Pages 70-71

J. P. Guilford and Creativity Testing. Joy Paul Guilford (who died in 1987) was an American psychologist best remembered for his psychometric analysis of human intelligence, especially the distinction between convergent and divergent thinking. His work suggested that with the proper tests, we could measure the ability and perhaps the tendency of an individual mind to seek out and propose multiple and even unusual answers to a prompt. Part of the problem with the tests that were created specifically to measure divergent cognition is that the relationship between divergent thinking and creative productivity was never established, and as a general rule, these tests failed to predict who would create a magical melody or a successful business venture. To read further, see Guilford's 1950 article

"Creativity" in *American Psychologist* or his book *The Nature of Human Intelligence* (1967).

Chapter 9

Pages 75–76

Charles Limb and Improvisation. The work of musician and neuroscientist Dr. Charles Limb can best be accessed via his TED talk on how the brains of jazz and rap artists function during performance. See https://www.ted.com/talks/charles_limb_your_brain_on_improv?language=en.

Chapter 10

Pages 86–87

Sources of the Paideia Coached Project. The Coached Project as presented here drew on insights from a number of school reform projects from the 1980s and '90s: the Coalition of Essential Schools, Foxfire, Understanding by Design, and Problem-Based Learning, as well as others. This work is based in part on *The Paideia Proposal* (1982) and *The Paideia Program* (1984), both written by philosopher Mortimer Adler and the original Paideia Group. To learn more about secondary influences, such as the Coalition of Essential Schools, read the series of Horace books by Ted Sizer, beginning with *Horace's Compromise* (1984), as well as *The New American High School* (2013). To delve into the Foxfire project, read the series of Foxfire books (the first of which appeared in 1972) written by students at Rabun Gap-Nacoochee School (https://www.foxfire.org/shop/category/books/) as well as Eliot Wigginton's *Sometimes a Shining Moment: The Foxfire Experience* (1985). For more on Understanding by Design, see Grant Wiggins and Jay McTighe's book by the same title (1998), as well as other work by McTighe and Wiggins. Problem-Based Learning (or PBL) is an international, student-centered pedagogical movement in which students learn about a subject by working as a team to solve open-ended problems. It was originally developed for use in medical education.

Pages 90–91

Academies for the Arts. There are numerous examples of schools and colleges dedicated to teaching the arts. One of the most interesting is the University of North Carolina School of the Arts in Winston-Salem, North

Carolina. UNCSA is a public coeducational arts conservatory that grants high school, undergraduate, and graduate degrees. Founded in 1963 as the North Carolina School of the Arts by then-governor Terry Sanford and based on the vision of novelist John Ehle, it was the first public arts conservatory in the United States. Programs offered by the conservatory—including but not limited to dance, drama, and film—are widely recognized as some of the best programs across the world. The school owns and operates the Stevens Center in downtown Winston-Salem as a performance space. Despite its affiliation with the University of North Carolina system, UNCSA offers a full high school program for students gifted in the arts. A number of elements make UNCSA especially intriguing: its democratic stature as a "public" school, its emphasis on authentic performance rather than standardized testing, and its dedication to providing students the opportunity to do what they love in the most rigorous environment possible (see https://www.uncsa.edu/). For the story of its early years, see Leslie Banner's *A Passionate Preference: The Story of the North Carolina School of the Arts* (1987).

Chapter 11

Pages 97–98

Teacher as Coach. The idea of teacher as coach is not a new one; however, in the past, it generally meant one-on-one tutoring or counseling. This model is powerful but unrealistic for much of the school day. Strong teacher-coaches work with entire classes of students in most scenarios, which often means a true paradigm shift for academic instructors. In developing this pedagogical model, Paideia educators found it imperative that teachers reimagine themselves as engaged in the continuous learning of their craft, which included not only their teaching skills but also mastery of their subject. The role of the teacher in a Coached Project is like that of the master craftsperson (historian, scientist, writer, technician, mathematician, etc.) surrounded by apprentices. In their role as apprentices, the students work closely with the teacher and with the other apprentices to practice the various skills involved in producing the highest quality product or performance. To learn more about the teacher as model learner and master craftsperson, see *The Paideia Project: Creating Authentic Units of Study* (2nd edition, 2011).

Pages 103–04

Schools for Creativity. To further explore the American public schools and teachers that are already teaching for the future, read George H. Wood's *Schools that Work: America's Most Innovative Public Education Programs* (1992). As principal and later superintendent, George Wood led the innovations at Federal Hocking High School that are summarized here; in addition, he has long been one of America's most freethinking and visionary educators. For a more recent exploration of the same topic, see Ted Dintersmith's *What School Could Be: Insights and Inspiration from Teachers across America* (2018).

Chapter 12

Pages 108–09

Paideia Seminar. We define the Paideia (or Socratic) Seminar as a collaborative, intellectual dialogue facilitated by open-ended questions about a text. The seminar cycle features close reading of complex text followed by thoughtful speaking and listening in the seminar proper, culminating in the writing process. In this way, students practice the full range of literacy skills in concert. To read more about the use of seminar to teach critical and creative thinking, see *Teaching Critical Thinking: Using Seminars for 21st Century Literacy* (2012) by Terry Roberts and Laura Billings. For an introduction to planning and facilitating effective seminars, see *The Paideia Seminar: Creative Thinking Through Dialogue* (3rd edition, 2019).

REFERENCES

Adler, Mortimer J., and Charles Van Doren. *How to Read a Book.* New York: Simon & Schuster, 1972.

Adler, Mortimer J. *The Paideia Program.* New York: Macmillan, 1984.

Adler, Mortimer J. *The Paideia Proposal: An Educational Manifesto.* New York: Macmillan, 1982.

American Psychological Association (APA) Presidential Task Force on Psychology in Education. *Learner-Centered Psychological Principles: Guidelines for School Redesign and Reform.* 1993.

Armstrong, Thomas. *Multiple Intelligences in the Classroom.* 4th ed. Alexandria, VA: ASCD, 2018.

Bakewell, Sarah. *How to Live: Or A Life of Montaigne in One Question and Twenty Attempts at an Answer.* New York: Other Press, 2010.

Banner, Leslie. *A Passionate Preference: The Story of the North Carolina School of the Arts.* Winston-Salem, NC: North Carolina School of the Arts Foundation, 1987.

Barzun, Jacques. *The Culture We Deserve.* Middletown, CT: Wesleyan University Press, 1989.

Barzun, Jacques. *From Dawn to Decadence: 1500 to the Present: 500 Years of Western Cultural Life.* New York: Harper, 2000.

Brandt, Anthony, and David Eagleman. *The Runaway Species: How Human Creativity Remakes the World.* New York: Catapult, 2017.

Brooks, David. "The Rise of the Amphibians." *New York Times,* February 15, 2018.

Childress, Herb. "Seventeen Reasons Why Football Is Better Than High School." *Phi Delta Kappan* 79.8 (1998): 616–19.

Claxton, Guy. *Hare Brain, Tortoise Mind: Why Intelligence Increases When You Think Less.* New York: Ecco, 1997.

Csikszentmihalyi, Mihaly. *Flow: The Psychology of Optimal Experience.* New York: Harper, 1990.

Davidson, Cathy N. *The New Education: How to Revolutionize the University to Prepare Students for a World in Flux*. New York: Basic Books, 2017.

Dietrich, Arne. "The Cognitive Neuroscience of Creativity." *Psychonomic Bulletin & Review* 11.6 (2004): 1011–1026.

Dintersmith, Ted. *What School Could Be: Insights and Inspiration from Teachers Across America*. Princeton, NJ: Princeton University Press, 2018.

Durant, Will, and Ariel Durant. *The Lessons of History*. New York: Simon & Schuster, 1968.

Emerson, Ralph Waldo. "Self-Reliance" in *Essays, First Series*, 1841.

Ferguson, Niall. *Civilization: The West and the Rest*. New York: Penguin, 2011.

Friedman, Thomas L. *Hot, Flat, and Crowded: Why the World Needs a Green Revolution—And How We Can Renew Our Global Culture*. Updated and Expanded. New York: Penguin, 2009.

Friedman, Thomas L. *The World Is Flat: A Brief History of the Twenty-First Century*. New York: Farrar, Straus and Giroux, 2005.

Gardner, Howard. *Creating Minds: An Anatomy of Creativity Seen through the Lives of Freud, Einstein, Picasso, Stravinsky, Eliot, Graham, and Gandhi*. New York: Basic Books, 1993.

Gardner, Howard. *Frames of Mind: The Theory of Multiple Intelligences*. New York: Basic Books, 1983.

Gardner, Howard. *The Mind's New Science: A History of the Cognitive Revolution*. New York: Basic Books, 1987.

Gardner, Howard. *The Unschooled Mind: How Children Think and How Schools Should Teach*. New York: Basic Books, 1991.

Gladwell, Malcolm. *Outliers: The Story of Success*. New York: Little, Brown, 2008.

Goodwin, Doris Kearns. *No Ordinary Time: Franklin and Eleanor Roosevelt: The Home Front in World War II*. New York: Simon & Schuster, 1994.

Guilford, J. P. "Creativity." *American Psychologist* 5.9 (1950): 444–54.

Guilford, J. P. *The Nature of Human Intelligence*. New York: McGraw-Hill, 1967.

Herodotus. *The Great Books of the Western World*, vol. 6. Trans. George Rawlinson. Chicago: University of Chicago Press, 1952.

Hobbes, Thomas. *Leviathan or the Matter, Form and Power of a Commonwealth Ecclesiastical and Civil.* Originally published 1651. *Great Books of the Western World*, vol. 23. Chicago: Encyclopedia Britannica, 1952.

Hutchins, Robert Maynard. *The Great Conversation: The Substance of a Liberal Education.* Chicago: Encyclopedia Britannica, 1952.

Isaacson, Walter. *The Innovators: How a Group of Hackers, Geniuses, and Geeks Created the Digital Revolution.* New York: Simon & Schuster, 2014.

Isaacson, Walter. *Leonardo da Vinci.* New York: Simon & Schuster, 2017.

Keats, John. *Selected Letters.* Ed. Robert Gittings. New York: Oxford University Press, 2009.

Lao Tzu (Laozi). *Tao Te Ching.* Trans. Chad Hansen. New York: Metro, 2009.

National Paideia Center. *The Paideia Project: Creating Authentic Units of Study.* Chapel Hill, NC: National Paideia Center, 2011.

National Paideia Center. *The Paideia Seminar: Creative Thinking Through Dialogue.* Asheville, NC: National Paideia Center, 2019.

Pinker, Steven. *The Better Angels of Our Nature: Why Violence Has Declined.* New York: Viking, 2011.

Pinker, Steven. *Enlightenment Now.* New York: Penguin, 2018.

Pinker, Steven. *The Stuff of Thought: Language as a Window into Human Nature.* New York: Viking, 2007.

Powell, Arthur G., Eleanor Farrar, and David K. Cohen. *The Shopping Mall High School: Winners and Losers in the Educational Marketplace.* New York: Houghton Mifflin, 1985.

Roberts, Terry, and Laura Billings. *Teaching Critical Thinking: Using Seminars for 21st Century Literacy.* Larchmont, NY: Eye on Education, 2012.

Robinson, Ken, and Lou Aronica. *Creative Schools: The Grassroots Revolution That's Transforming Education.* New York: Viking, 2015.

Sacks, Oliver. *The River of Consciousness.* New York: Knopf, 2017.

Sizer, Theodore R. *Horace's Compromise: The Dilemma of the American High School.* Boston & New York: Houghton Mifflin, 1984.

Sizer, Theodore R. *The New American High School.* San Francisco: Jossey-Bass, 2013.

Spencer, Elizabeth. *Starting Over.* New York: Norton, 2014.

Tharp, Twyla. *The Creative Habit: Learn It and Use It for Life*. New York: Simon & Schuster, 2006.

Watts, Edward J. *Mortal Republic: How Rome Fell into Tyranny*. New York: Basic Books, 2018.

Whyte, William H. *The Organization Man*. New York: Simon & Schuster, 1956.

Wiggins, Grant, and Jay McTighe. *Understanding by Design*. Alexandria, VA: ASCD, 1998.

Wigginton, Eliot. *Sometimes a Shining Moment: The Foxfire Experience*. Garden City, NY: Anchor Books, 1986.

Wood, George. *Schools that Work: America's Most Innovative Public Education Programs*. New York: Dutton, 1992.

INDEX

ACKNOWLEDGMENTS

This book grew out of an evocative conversation with Howard Gardner that took place over lunch in Cambridge several years ago. I had just reread his fine book, *Creating Minds: An Anatomy of Creativity Seen Through the Lives of Freud, Einstein, Picasso, Stravinsky, Eliot, Graham, and Ghandi*, so I was primed when the conversation turned to the role of creativity in 21st century life. I owe a great debt to Howard, not just for his decades of paradigm-shifting work, but also for this germ of an idea. As we agreed that day, I wrote the book and Howard wrote the foreward.

I am also grateful to my colleagues at the National Paideia Center, Jeremy Spielman and Valerie Shrader, as well as the numerous Paideia educators who have contributed to the development of this book through their good work. Together, we represent an international family of teachers dedicated to the dream of a public education that is at once rigorous and equitable.

Once the ideas began to take shape, the team at Turner Publishing--especially Stephanie Beard—responded to the project with an enthusiasm and encouragement that hasn't abated to this day.

Special thanks, as well, to Wendy Ikoku for reading the various manuscript versions of *The New Smart* with her painstaking eye and questioning mind.

And to my son Henry Roberts for discussing and debating chapter by chapter, the ideas shared in this book, providing a twenty-something perspective to his sixty-something father.

This book is dedicated to Henry along with his brother Jesse and sister Margaret—three thrilling examples of the creative mind and heart. Together, they give us hope as well as inspiration.

And finally, of course, a deep bow to Lynn, who had to revisit these ideas over countless suppertime conversations. Bless her for patience beyond that of Job.

ABOUT THE AUTHOR

Dr. Terry Roberts is a lifelong teacher and educational reformer as well as an award-winning novelist. As a student of intellectual history, he is fascinated by the power of dialogue to inspire critical and creative thinking. Since 1992, he has been the director of the National Paideia Center, a school reform organization dedicated to making intellectual rigor accessible to all children. He has written extensively about public education, notably *The Power of Paideia Schools*, *The Paideia Classroom*, and *Teaching Critical Thinking: Using Seminars for 21st Century Literacy* (with Laura Billings). In addition, he is the author of three celebrated novels: *A Short Time to Stay Here* (winner of the Willie Morris Award for Southern Fiction); *That Bright Land* (winner of the Thomas Wolfe Memorial Literary Award and the James Still Award for Writing about the Appalachian South); and most recently, *The Holy Ghost Speakeasy and Revival*.

Roberts lives in Asheville, North Carolina, with his wife, Lynn. He has three children: Jesse, Margaret, and Henry.